What the Heart Already Knows

What the Heart Already Knows

Stories of Advent, Christmas, and Epiphany

Phyllis A. Tickle

Illustrated by
Jim Bateman

The Upper Room
Nashville, Tennessee

What the Heart Already Knows

Copyright © 1985 by Phyllis A. Tickle.
All rights reserved.

All scripture quotations are from the King James Version of the Bible.

"Noel, Holy Mother" has previously appeared in *The City Essays & Country Editions* published by Dixie Flyer Press and in *The Episcopalian* (December 1984).

Cover Design: *Steve Laughbaum*
Book Design: *Thelma Whitworth*
First Printing: *September, 1985* (10)

Library of Congress Catalog Card Number: 85-51242
ISBN 0-8358-0522-0

Printed in the United States of America

CONTENTS

Religion has always kept earth time.
Liturgy only gives sanction to what
the heart already knows.

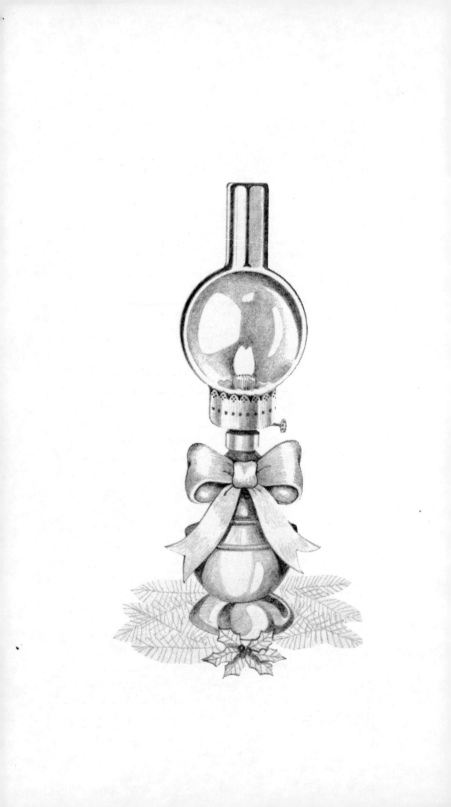

PROLOGUE

The essays in this book concern themselves with the three liturgical seasons and with eleven of the holy days which in lay terms and for convenience we usually call simply "Christmas." Since its beginning, however, the church has separated Advent from Christmas, and both from the season of the Epiphany.

The four Sundays which precede Christmas Day itself are the calendar by which we mark the passing of the Advent season and the approach of the Christmas one. These have traditionally been times of retreat and introspection for Christians—if no longer to think penitentially on our sins, at least to consider with godly fear and joy the blending of our life into divine process.

In the church's scheme of things, Christmas as such begins, and Advent ends, with the birth of Our Lord. The Feast of the Nativity is usually celebrated by most Christians, of course, on Christmas Eve and the midnight service. But regardless of whether we date it on the twenty-fourth of December or the twenty-fifth, its joy becomes increasingly private over the course of our years, individualized into each heart so completely as to be almost universal and beyond the need of the telling.

The twelve days of Christmas come to an end on January 6, and the season of the Epiphany begins. But Epiphany not only ends Christmas; it also fulfills it by celebrating the revelation of the Christ to the whole world. The coming of Incarnate God to all people, especially to those of us who are by race Gentiles, is the bridge from birth into life, the event that makes Easter possible for most of us. The light of the Epiphany illuminates the church's year as it illuminates the human races from whom the kings came.

Holy seasons, like holy days, were not so much invented by the church as they were invented by life itself, I think. By common consent we hold to and preserve that which living has shown us contains the truths of both humankind and God.

I am not a cleric. I have never wanted to study in a seminary or even to have access to one. I am instead a layperson, a writer and editor by trade, a woman. Over my fifty-odd years of living in cities and villages, mill towns and on farms, I have come increasingly to think that every believer must be a kind of psalmist, either literally or privately. That living itself has been given, at least in part, as a way of knowing God intimately. Every event takes on significance in that context, for there is no waste in experience. Every man and woman we meet becomes a metaphor of ourselves; every event, a simile; every thing, a symbol.

As Christians we are taught that our collective understanding and knowledge over the centuries since the coming of God have become, and are contained in, the liturgy and ritual of the church herself, the body of Christ passing itself on to each new member—part in the spiritual codes of symbol and sacrament, ritual and saint. Increasingly I find hope of the shared symbol's becoming once more the common language by which we rear our young, and the mother tongue by which we all will someday cut the lines that separate us from one another.

The essays which follow are true in that they factually report what has happened to me and my family during the days of many Advents, Christmases, and Epiphanies past. I hope they are true to the mark also in that, in retelling one family's progress toward liturgical truth, they will represent the progress of many, many families toward that same understanding.

We live in a culture still too new to yet have defined itself and under a government so young that my own lifetime has spanned a quarter of its history. In such times and circumstances I have found, in the heritage of the church, a transcendant purpose and connectedness for my own part of creation. For that I have always been grateful, both at Christmas and throughout the years. This book is dedicated to the hope that it may be so also for my own children and for those fellow Christians for whom Christianity is both our past and our future.

First Sunday of Advent

Thanksgiving has never seemed real at our house. Last spring we had Easter and it was real, as if all of history and all of nature had agreed to do the thing in unison. Since then we have partitioned our time with Independence Day and Labor Day, Halloween and Thanksgiving—pleasant interruptions, long on food and drink but short on connectedness with humanity outside America.

But each year, almost before the last slice of mincemeat pie is gone, I can feel the activity accelerating—the real thing comes next! John wants to fetch the Advent wreath. Sam, Jr. wants the Advent calendar hung a week ahead of time. Rebecca wants to set the music out on the piano rack. The earth subtly joins in their agitation. The berries redden on the haw bushes. The holly grows thorny and turgid. The cold comes and the animals rest platonically close to each other.

The autumn is dying, as we all will die, and the days shorten into their ending. What and who will survive the cold and the dark will only be known four months hence when spring and the Easter light return. Whatever does survive will be changed, reshaped by the cold, reborn after deep sleep—acorn to sapling, larva to insect, God to flesh, time to forever.

It's coming, the mystery among us, and we begin the marking of most ancient time. The first Sunday of Advent, over the centuries, has come to honor Isaiah and his place as the first prophet to foretell the promise of an Incarnate Yahweh. Now all the earth once again awaits the coming of Christ.

1

THIS VINING WREATH

December already! Hard to believe, despite the lowering sky and the silent earth all around us. Tomorrow would be the first Sunday in Advent—"Isaiah's Sunday" we call it at our house because the church liturgy is always drawn from that rich and regal man—and because of the wreath, of course. But the nine-year-old is not concerned with Isaiah himself this afternoon, nor with matters liturgical. She just wants to begin the wreath.

Her brothers have already brought the brass Advent wreath down from the attic and set it in place on the dinner table, and she has seen to getting the candles firmly in place—the three purple and the single pink one for Gaudete Sunday. Together they have taped the Advent calendar in place on the big window in the kitchen so that the half light of December can the better illuminate its charming little tissue chambers of toys and goodies and medieval fancies.

All is ready for Christmas to begin except for the wreath. Her agitation that we finish this last and most intricate of our tasks is contagious. Ultimately, for me as for all parents, it is easier to give in to her urgency than to try to work any longer around it. We bundle scarves around us, put on our farm gloves, and go to gather the grapevines.

She has spent all the week inspecting the leafless, twining branches and has clearly fixed in her mind the lengths she wants to cut—the ones that Daddy has approved our cutting and the ones she covets for their excessive tendrils and pliable thickness.

She bounces around me like a cocker spaniel, showing more little-girlness in this task than we have seen in months from her. There will not be many more Christmases when this ritual will excite her. Secretly, I am surprised to realize, I look forward to the time when she does not want to help with this one part of Christmas. She is the last of our seven, and with her leaving, this work will be mine in solitude and in reverie. Standing in front of a vine and watching her pleasure, I am in no hurry for that day to come, only quietly content that someday it will and that this most mysterious part of the holy season will be mine again.

"My well-beloved hath a vineyard in a very fruitful hill." That's Isaiah 5. "Now will I sing to my well-beloved a song of my beloved touching his vineyard." Well, my well-beloved has a vineyard too, except it's more an arbor than a vineyard. And we have it not for the wine but for reasons I have never quite been able to discuss with him.

The arbor is a rustic contrivance made of cedar posts and crossbeams that have, over the years, weathered into a sedate presence that sets a tone of nineteenth century rurality for the whole back of our farm. Its construction was the first personal act of our coming to this land. As soon as we had finished the absolutely necessary like repairing the fence and the absolutely odious like re-siding the barn and running electricity to it, Sam, without so much as a by-your-leave, began to dig post holes around the patio.

He began right at the back door and proceeded around the whole, even around the outdoor barbeque pit, until he had wrapped the patio and its environs in uprights and come all the way back again to the other side of the kitchen door. The posts were followed the next day by crossbeams which were in turn followed by meticulous cultivation of the earth underneath and finally by the arrival of the vines ordered out of the Perkins catalog.

It was three weeks from the uprights to my discovery of what he was about. When I asked him why we had to have the grapes right up under foot that way, his answer was simply that one had to be able to be near them. I was innocent, if no longer young, and I had never been involved with grapes before. What I did not then understand but now realize is that the degree of intimacy he was talking about is the same one which causes folks to put the baby's nursery next to the master bedroom.

Despite my lack of personal commitment to their cause, the grapes came up anyway, of course. Everything always grows profusely for Sam, so nobody was especially surprised about the grapes doing so.

During the next summer, the vines reached the height of the first crosstie and the incredible process began—Daddy's absorption with the grapes. Such workings of the soil around the roots. Such care in the mixing of the fertilizer. Such exquisite pruning and lifting up of tendrils—each one set up on its crosspiece as tenderly as a child is lifted to the countertop to watch the baking. In the cool of the July and August

15

evenings, the grapes became the source of hours of conversation and companionship.

By the end of the second summer the grapes had made a cloister of the patio. No breeze moved there— the leaves and vines were too tight a wall to admit of that—but ten thousand leaves breathed out moisture and oxygen into the enclosed space and an enormous peace pervaded the place in the late twilights. Sitting on the glider watching him work, I could see only the white of his hands in the half-dark and the intensity of his face.

"What are you thinking about?" he asked.

I couldn't have told him, even after all these years together, that I was thinking about his hands, a lover's hands among the vines. So I said, "Nothing" and watched night after summer night.

In the third summer of the arbor there grew up a strange vine—probably, he said, from a grafting that was wild. It was mean and scrawny and demanding. He pruned it back to the place on the branch where it had burst forth. It came again. He cut it back. The process went on and on, Sam and the wild vine.

Then one evening, as I sat dreaming on the glider, he came around the corner of the arbor with the mattock in his hand, and I watched mesmerized as he delivered blow after blow at the roots themselves. They were not the blows of removal; they were the blows of rage. The mattock rose and fell, rose and fell, long after the offending plant itself was severed from the soil and from any hope of life. Then the vine was, with great precision and detail, totally removed, tendril by tendril, from the frame of the arbor.

The whole was then taken to the garbage barrel— the most astonishing act of the whole episode. A thousand times I had heard him say to the boys about their prunings and clippings, "Throw them over into the pasture. Give back what you have taken." Not so with the vine. It was to be denied life forever, to be burned at the dump with the rest of our refuse. It is one of my more solemn memories of those early years on the farm.

"And now, O inhabitants of Jerusalem, and men of Judah, judge, I pray you, betwixt me and my vineyard. What could have been done more to my vineyard, that I have not done in it?" Isaiah 5 again.

It was that fall also that we made the first juice from the grapes. Of all the labor and routine of the farm, the grapes were the only thing Sam had never asked me to help with, had obviously never wanted me to contribute to, and it was so also with the harvesting and juicing. He gathered the bunches. He sorted the fruit. He rendered the juice and seasoned it. I was fascinated.

In time I came to realize that no other part of what we do on the land so completely tests one's skill and acumen at husbandry. Here, one mistake in growing ruins the whole crop, not just one vine. And here, one mistake in sorting renders the juice just a shade beyond ruby, just a faint texture into cloudy, just a taste toward adulterated. Of all the things we grow, only this one demands excellence in each member part of the vat load, demands total accuracy in selection.

That year the juice was declared delicious by bright children who knew what to say, but it was not translucent, and there was no lying that fact away.

The next year was a different story, however. The vines thrived in the unusually warm summer months, growing lush and full to bursting as August waxed warm and breathless around us. Rebecca, like me forbidden to tend or even touch the vines, was old enough to desire the denied. She spent all of early August bringing me daily reports on which bunches were going to be ready first, which bird had dared to approach the cat-filled patio, which tendrils Daddy really ought to clip if he were smart. We never shared any of her wisdom with the vineyard keeper, of course, but he must have sensed her absorption, for he let her watch him finally as he cut the bunches and he let her carry some of them into the kitchen.

That year the juice was indeed perfect—translucent, pure ruby, and sweet when Sam offered me the first pouring. "In that day sing ye unto her, a vineyard of red wine. I the Lord do keep it; I will water it every moment: lest *any* hurt it, I will keep it night and day" (Isa. 27:2-3).

That was the year we made the first wreath from the vines. It was almost an accident. Sam cut away the branches he wanted pruned back, and the boys dutifully were picking up the prunings when John began to twist his collection to hold it better. Abruptly he stopped, looked at what he had done, and began to deliberately fashion a circle. In short order Sam, Jr. perceived what was happening, went in for some jute, and within minutes had begun to lash his brother's circle into our Christmas wreath. We got better at it, of course, in time. The next year after that there was less jute showing and more tendril. Now we do it without giving much thought to the craft of the thing, only to its meaning.

I was alone that first Christmas when I carried their accidental wreath around the house to the front door and hung it there. Looking at it, I could still see the moving whiteness of Sam's hands as he had tended it in the twilights of so many evenings; could still taste my shock at his anger as he beat out the intruding wild vine that had threatened it; could still hear the words of the ancient prophecy—"And there shall come forth a rod out of the stem of Jesse, and a Branch shall grow out of his roots" (Isa. 11:1).

I went into the house and instead of the red ribbon I had intended, on impulse I picked up a spindle of white grosgrain from the sewing chest. Back outside, I wove the white in and out of the vine and then tied the whole into a full bow. Standing there I heard Rebecca's voice behind me.

"Why'd you put white on the Christmas wreath?"

I heard my own voice answering her from out of the depth of years. "Because it's not a Christmas wreath. It's an Isaiah wreath."

And the holy season has always begun so for us in all the years since.

Second Sunday of Advent

On the second Sunday of Advent, Christendom hears from its pulpits and its lectionaries the words of St. John the Baptizer. John's was the voice of one crying in the wilderness, the last proclaimer of Our Lord before his coming into history and the only one of his prophets to actually see and worship him.

If God were at play when creating the universe in much the same way that we create dreams from and of ourselves, and if God became enchanted with the creature thus created—indeed so charmed by it as to grant it life beyond the game—then John stands as the bridge between God's love for the creature and God's gift of life to it.

In two weeks, life will enter into the game's rules in order to leave itself amongst the players. But of all those who carried the promise to us, only John was witness to its fulfillment; and by next Sunday the process will already be in place again in the womb of a virgin.

2

WHAT WENT YE OUT TO SEE?

"What went ye out into the wilderness for to see?" (Luke 7:24) It's Christ's ancient question about John the Baptizer, but it always plagues my early Decembers as if I were hearing it each year for the first time.

"There is not a greater prophet than John the Baptist: but he that is least in the kingdom of God is greater than he" (Luke 7:28). How eternally unfair that always seemed to me when I was a child. I would mourn through all of Advent for John and for all the other human entities that served salvation without owning it on earth.

"What went ye out into the wilderness for to see?" I also wrestle the question annually because Christmas is coming; and whatever else Christmas may be, it is surely the one time of year when everyone celebrates the rurality in which I daily live. For the folks of Herod's era the search may indeed have been for a prophet. "Yea, I say unto you, and much more than a prophet" (Luke 7:26). For us—for me and my family—the trek to the wilderness was a journey to broader focus.

Originally, of course, it was the heavens and their citizenry who first brought us back to the farm. Having spent most of my own late childhood and early adolescence walking around with my face up and my head parallel to the ground, I early and unconsciously gained some simple sense of the sky as place. In a way, I suppose, my playmates and I domesticated the heavens as innocently as we domesticated our earth space.

That the skies changed disposition and color was as natural to us as it was that the land around our feet should shift with the seasons, should follow a reassuringly predictable cycle, should shed one fascination for another. We watched the boiling clouds for snow in winter and counted thunderheads in summer, telling our seasons as simply as most children tell their dreams.

At night our eyes walked a dome which was as familiar as our own bedrooms in the dark. Finding Orion each evening and counting the jewels in his belt was not mythology, it was personalized fact. Watching the bears rotate with the passing winter was as much an evidence that the system was working in proper order as was awaking to the lengthening daylight. The one of us children who first spotted Venus each March was guaranteed to be lucky all that year. Such good fortune was, quite literally, written in the stars for us.

When, as a bride and groom, Sam and I moved to the city thirty years ago, neither of us really noticed at first that our world immediately shrank to half its usual size. The buildings were tall and blocked even the daytime view of much, but they were also exhilarating in a way that the tall trees of home had never been. The red maples and oaks and pines of our childhood had stood high, right enough, but they had also become bent and crooked and bowed at the whim of the winds and in accord with their need for sustenance. The buildings of the city were a different matter.

Fully adult by then, I felt, when I lifted my face up and set my head parallel to the ground, a surge of glory which I had never felt under the trees. City dwellers may joke about the gawkers and hicks who keep looking up when they visit urban centers, but the emotion is very intense. The buildings are not the marvel—or they weren't for me. The people who built them are the marvel. Even now, when I have been into our city or have been visiting some other one, I have an enormous need to praise human ingenuity. How cunning and grand is our skill, our sheer technical acumen, our conceptual power. Any person who can stand in the middle of a corridor of skyscrapers and not look up is cynical beyond endurance, in my opinion. And any man or woman who can look up from such a vantage point and not rejoice in his or her own humanness is dull beyond salvation.

So Sam and I gave up much of our accustomed heavens in exchange for the beauty of an interrupted and arranged sky, one for which angles and lines served as unbending frame and artful enhancement. The night sky we lost completely to that other urban wonder—arc lighting—an electric event that still thrills me when I am in any city after nightfall.

The birds in the city were a different matter and their absence was obvious from the very first. The number of birds who are willing to share interrupted sky with humanity and live on fast-food throw-aways is limited. Even more regrettably, what birds there were were little! The biggest bird I ever saw in the years we lived in the city was a hoot owl and he looked distressed the whole ten hours he spent with us as he was passing through.

And except for that one-night stand of the hoot owl, our city birds were singularly quiet. Whatever that noise is that pigeons make, it will not hold a candle to the enthusiasm of a guinea hen whose territory is being invaded or to the love song of a peacock.

So almost ten years ago, when we had finally arrived at that stage of our professional lives and at that level of overpopulation (there were seven young Tickles by then as well as two old ones) which permitted or required us to leave the city for farm life again, it was the sky that gave me my first rush of nostalgia, poignancy, and joy.

On the day before we were to move in, I drove out to open the house, turn on the appliances, prepare for the van and the children. As I stepped out of the car, I felt it immediately—the heaviness oppressing everything, the silvered undersides of the oak and maple leaves turned over skyward, the clouds roaring over the flat fields instead of flowing casually above the course of the river. All the instincts of my childhood revived. Always trust the sky!

I ran in, opening doors and windows as I went. Then, braced against the brick wall of the garage, I watched. Up the road it came, turning almost at right angles to tear up the pine at the foot of the drive. It followed the fence line, skirted mercifully around the house and cut left into the orchard, taking two more trees in its wake. Behind it, the sky settled and the rain began. I stood there in the garage and cried with a child's joy over that small tornado. It was the sign; I was home again at last.

That first summer I sat for hours every night on the

patio or in the field and watched the stars wheel and burn and do the thing they have always done in just the way that they have always done it. My sense of settling in and belonging again was directly tied not only to my renewed intimacy with the weather but also with my ability to find Orion every night. (I must confess that young John beat me to Venus that first year. It didn't matter; I felt lucky and blessed anyway.)

While I was content with the clouds and the trees and the stars, Sam was miserable without the birds. Within a month of our arrival he had put in chickens. There is no more unpleasant a creature than a chicken. Some of my unhappiest memories from early childhood have to do with chickens. Being flogged time and again by my pet rooster. Cleaning up the flagstones after my father had wrung the neck of Sunday dinner and let it flop around the backyard until it died. Hauling eggs door-to-door to the neighbors who wisely bought ours rather than raising their own—and washing the distressing things before I hauled them, for that matter!

I was firmly opposed to chickens and had said so before we moved. Nonetheless and with no evidence of shame or betrayal, Sam bought baby chicks at the hatchery, and within six months we had full-grown and randomly airborne chickens. I was chagrined to realize, that spring when the first brown eggs came into the kitchen, that I really liked brown eggs better than white and that all that noise and flapping around out back were really very pleasant.

Then we added the guineas. We put them in as watchdogs originally. A guinea belongs to one set of people and God help his nonfamily. The first time the power and water man came to read the meter, the whole north end of the county knew we had put in guineas. The poor man never did get an accurate reading and we were estimated for months until we got a new and more rural meter man.

The turkeys came next. A pair who changed each year but whom we invariably named Christmas and Thanksgiving. The children raised them as pets with a certain ferocious sadism, since there was no question in anybody's mind each year about where the two were to end up. As soon as the chicks were large enough to leave the turkey lot, they were allowed to roam during the day, foraging where they wished and gobbling at will.

At night, Sam, Jr., who has the biggest appetite in the family and therefore the greatest interest in turkeys, always had the chore of catching them and setting each up on the roof of the smokehouse to perch for the night. It was with enormous relief each August or early September when he could finally announce to his father that the birds were at last big enough to roost by themselves.

The geese came in our first fall. They landed, a flying "V" of five of them, on the pond below the house and spent three days with us. The children were ecstatic, but fearful of alarming them. Despite my assurance that the geese would not startle if one were reasonable, the children held back at the fence line, paralyzed by the wonder of the gift and by their anxiety lest it be snatched away before they were done with it. And, of course, the geese did go. But each year they have come back. We will hear them honking overhead in the spring and the fall and, looking up, see them as they bank and turn to land on the pond.

The great horned owl who took up residency with us was welcomed like an old and much needed friend, especially by Sam who would have built that

bird a private aviary had he asked for one. Great horned owls are not only extremely impressive, they are also murder on rats, of which our barn always seems to have more than its fair share. The bats of August I could live without except for their breathtaking swoops, but the barn swallows are the joy of our late summer evenings. Never was there a more graceful bird than that slender glider of feathers and daring.

The egrets come in from the Mississippi twice each year. I had never seen such creatures before our settling here. The first time the children came screaming in the back door wanting us to "Come quick!" I had no idea what it was we were looking at. The whole lower pasture was white with hundreds of birds resting on the brown stubble. A few dozen would rise and resettle, then another group would shift position—a sea of whitecaps undulating for hours that first fall before they flew away. Now we expect them each spring and each fall and predict, somewhat inaccurately, the intensity of the coming season by how early or late the egrets arrive.

The golden eagle who migrates through here on his way to the breeding grounds north of us at the Reelfoot sanctuary has become more and more of a lodger and less and less of a migrant. Last spring he must have stayed in our dead tree and soared over our fields for close to two weeks before he finally pushed on to his biological duty. John has learned how to call the eagle and I won't be terribly surprised when some spring he manages to entice that glowing creature into the backyard itself.

Which gets us to the ducks, both wild and domestic. Since we have a fowl yard full of domestic ducks, the wild ones seem perfectly willing to pay social calls from time to time and one is never sure at any given moment just how many ducks there are in the pen. But the wild ones also leave and go wherever it is that ducks go while the domestic ones, although they fly in and out, never migrate. As turkey-growing has become less interesting to the children, we have switched to ducks for our holiday fare.

In fact, to be perfectly honest, I am sure I think about all these philosophical matters during Advent in no small part because duck feathers rise and float all over my kitchen every time anyone opens the back door in December. And admittedly I give some thought to it all because in the thinner air of winter, the pines are greener outside, the berries brighter, and the nights skies more crystalline with their stars and planets. But basically I still think on them primarily because of John the Baptist and his wilderness.

I look around me at the hardness of our way of life: at the difficulty of growing and preserving what could more easily be bought; at the silliness of being twenty miles from the city where Sam practices medicine and in which at least some of my professional assignments must be completed; at the vulnerability of being, during much of each day, miles from any human help. But, even acknowledging all of that, I know again in each December that we can live no other way.

I still feel, even after all these years, that same wash of pride and grandeur when I see a huge city or stand among skyscrapers. No rush of glory comes for me here, not among these low sheds and two-rail fences. There is little about rural living that is inspiring.

But sitting here at my desk off the kitchen, watching at least three dozen pinfeathers as they run around on my clean floor, I know that it is the disorder of it all which makes the difference. In the city with its certain borders and its arranged structures, I observe life. Here I am life, one among equals. I matter less to myself out here where I am sealed in the center of life as purely as the yolk is sealed within the egg.

We don't have John the Baptizer any more. He's gone headless into some limbo that I have never understood theologically and that will probably always lie beyond my comprehension, but we have his wilderness with its constant flux and its disorder. And within the next two weeks, all of us—city dweller and farm dweller, Christian and non-Christian—will try to wrap it around us.

We will bring the pines in to us. We will string everywhere tiny lights that "glow like millions of twinkling stars," as their boxes all will say. We will lay out straw and set miniature barns upon it, putting odorless cows and lintless sheep to rest inside each of them. We will tie little red birds onto tree branches and tape gold ones to packages. We will exchange red flowers with each other. Finally, near the last of it all, we will drag some magnificent conifer indoors and think its grandeur complete only when we have topped the whole with an angel whom none of us has ever seen.

And we will sleep, most of us, for close to two weeks wrapped in the pleasure of that wilderness disorder; knowing, however briefly each year, life instead of living; mattering, at least for a little while, so much less to ourselves. We will do these things until peace itself becomes a kind of forerunner, a herald. Even so, come, Lord Jesus!

Third Sunday of Advent

This day passes the mystery of God-in-flesh to the Virgin and celebrates her uses and her virtue as vehicle to Incarnate Lord. Called "Gaudete Sunday" by the ancients, its name means simply, "We praise Thee," name and purpose being in harmony. While the other three candles in the Advent wreath are penitentially purple, Mary's candle is pink, bespeaking her ladyship and her joy.

3

NOEL, HOLY MOTHER

In the weak December light the bed sits in front of the double windows, a disheveled wad of blankets and quilts, a sea of wrinkles still warm from our bodies. As always, I begin setting off the pillows to fluff them and pulling the bottom sheet taut again. I lay back the covers to air, my hands moving in and out of the night's warmth and a life's memories. For twenty-five years we have slept here. We conceived nine children on this bed and brought seven of them to birth. Here I always rested afterwards. And here they have continued to join us in the morning, cold bare feet and knobby little knees hammering, inno-cent as Oedipus, against our mystery.

A shuttle of clouds blows over the lemony sun out-side, and the gray pattern swims across the exposed sheets, moves up the bedroom wall, and disappears on the ceiling. The wind is too cold today, and I draw the drapes shut, blocking both the light and the cold for a while longer.

So it begins again, the dying of our year. The long nights I yearn toward; the stripped trees and tan grasses; the greying of the sun. I tie a red ribbon around the lamp on the dresser. In a little while one of the children will bring a pine cone or a holly branch in from the field and slip it through the ribbon without my asking.

It is almost two weeks yet to the Holy Night, and I have much to do. But first I must pull the covers back up and smooth the spread. Always here, in this place of beginnings, is my center, the order of my day. This first, must be right. A pillow or two set just so and then on them the special one that says "Noel." "Birth." All over the world this fortnight people will wish each other birth; I will do it here.

This two weeks will be hard for me because they spend my dearest treasure. Our decorations and feasting are paid for with my privacy.

I will buy gifts for people I don't care about and think, however briefly, on the wonder of not buying gifts for some whom I deeply love. Loving me, they would think it a sham and reject both me and the thing I had bought. The children, too young still to know that distinction, will go through the stores, allowances in hand, and love for itself every gift they buy. Things belong in one's growing up or else one never overcomes the need of them somehow. So we will go and we will spend and we will have great joy, they in the doing and I in the not doing.

We will bring in the greens and the cones and consider (but not mention to each other) the dreary December. We will talk much in the kitchen about the bounty of the past summer's produce and cheerily assure each other that the whole thing will come again once the cold is over.

He and I will go out an evening or two and spend the money we have saved for this. Even more, we will

spend time—walking the aisles, buying gifts for the children we remember being. Then weary from so much travel through dimensions we usually respect, we will spend more time drinking coffee or chocolate in some little shop until it closes, and we will come home to this bed and the pleasure of sleeping with a stranger whom each of us only thought we knew.

Sometime in this two weeks I will put some extra money in the collection box for the children of Ethiopia and Cambodia, wishing it were more, knowing it cannot be. Sometime this two weeks he will write a check for the children of the Holy Land and one for those of Memphis, wishing it could be more, knowing it cannot be. Each one's children in their own place, in their own time; always the inequity.

We will go out each day and wish "Noel" to our friends and neighbors. We will attend open houses and drink eggnog from crystal cups. Before it is all over, we will dress a king or two to make his long trek, blue jeans under bathrobe, down an aisle or two. Knowing that he doesn't know why, we will make him do it anyway. In just a little while he will understand the painted gold and fake frankincense and weep for the wonder of it when his own son bears the eternal gifts down some other aisle. Time, that great mirage, pales before the truth of bathrobes and carols into the nothingness it is.

And I, as every year at this season, alone somewhere in some church or card shop or in front of some cheap, dime-store nativity, will stop before a plastic Madonna. Standing there, I will make a brief prayer to the memory of the real one who, like me, was highway to the world. Hers was the rapture of Magnificat and mine the fullness of pleasure, but it is our only difference. Ours together is the tearing of the flesh

35

and the pushing, forever the pushing out of the thing from the body into some other life.

So, Mary, even on Christmas morning, I will make this bed first, knowing that there has never really been anything other than this for you and me.

Noel, Holy Mother, Noel. It is time I went downstairs.

4

Fourth Sunday of Advent

The last Sunday before Christmas belongs to St. Joseph, and for centuries the fourth and last candle of the Advent wreath has been lighted by the father of the family, just as Sam will tonight light ours. As father and husband, it is he who in his earthly life is enjoined to be a metaphor and symbol of the divine One who grants life and protection to all things. But for my husband, as for my sons, it is increasingly a world in which the old virtues of strength and aggression and skill in physical prowess are no longer usable or useful. Living in rural America we hold to the last vestige of a life where traditional Josephs can exist in balance with their instincts and emotions.

Each year, like a coward, I am glad we personally have been spared the difficult transition to a new definition of fatherness, grateful for the farm life that delays the process beyond my own years, anxious for the boys gathered at our table for whom there will be no escape from change.

Each year, as the strong, blunt hands move across the table to light the final candle, I pray that those who have been created strong to war may grow strong for peace. With the lighting of the Joseph candle, Advent ends and Christmas nears. May peace on earth do likewise.

4

THE JOSEPH CANDLE

It had been the kind of autumn that year that dries the skins and crusts of everything. The wind, low and incessant across the open fields, daily sucked up any moisture the evening before had let fall. Now, deep into year's end, the sky had turned again. The winds had ceased and the rains had begun coming up from the South, Gulf water airborne up the valley of the Mississippi until just north of the Tennessee line where it hit frigid air and fell first as sleet, then as ice.

It was near the end of the third week of Advent when the storm began. The water we all had prayed for stung the windows and glazed the steps. By mid-afternoon of the first day I was sending the boys early to feed the stock. It would soon be too slick even for their youthful agility to safely move from house to cows and barn. Already ice-coated and glimmering in the gray sleet, the herd had begun that pitiable winter mooing with which they ask for the comfort of extra food.

Just at dusk we heard the first pine tree crack and fall into the abandoned garden. We would lose two more to the storm before the night was done with us.

By morning the roads were closed and the ice had turned to snow. Cattle to water, as well as feed. The boys groaned.

We salted the back steps and ate breakfast. By the time we were done, the salt and the last of the water from the teakettle had done the trick. No more excuses. Time to make it through the snow to the cows. Ax in hand, John headed grumbling toward the pond and Sam, Jr., with equal disgust, toward the hay loft. In less than half an hour, Sam came back in, rosy cheeked and happy. At twelve he still tended, once the odious chores were finished, to change back into a normal boy with acres of snow around him and no school.

After another ten minutes or so, John came wearily up the hill from the pond, dragging the ax behind him. There was no little boy here, just a tired man.

"That ice is at least four inches deep at the edge already."

He set the ax in the corner next to the back door and threw himself into the nearest kitchen chair, his hands half frozen even through his leather gloves.

By three o'clock that Saturday afternoon the snow had covered everything, turning the whole farm into a landscape of unreadable mounds and valleys. Once more the boys trudged early to their chores, this time with Daddy's help. The pond had frozen over again and the water hole had to be reopened. Shortly after supper was cleaned up, we all made our way to early beds, lulled as we usually are into that deep sleep which serious snow brings.

The next morning was the fourth and final Sunday of Advent, but there would be no church services for us nor for any in our rural parish. Life was still stopped—except for the cows! Sam, Jr. to the hay loft; John and Sam, Sr. to the pond; Rebecca and Mama to the stove. In due time the cattle were cared for and the men ready to eat.

"That ice is at least six inches thick down there this morning," was Sam's only comment as he sat down to drink his coffee.

I was finishing the sausage gravy when I looked out the kitchen window and saw the cows. Three of them, white and pathetic, were standing at the fence looking across the yard through the blowing snow to the house.

"Something must be wrong," I said. "The cows have come to the fence."

Too weary to worry about cows and too hungry to care, nobody at my breakfast table even responded. We ate and I got up to clear the table.

Through the kitchen window I saw six or seven cows, their heads over the top railing of the back fence. There were all looking straight at the house.

"Something's wrong!"

But John was having none of it. Nothing could be wrong. He and his father had just come in. What could be wrong?

"Go upstairs and tell your father to put his overalls back on. Something is wrong at the pond or the cows wouldn't have come up."

My voice sounded sharp even to me. Begrudgingly he went, and begrudgingly they both rebooted and edged down the back steps. I watched as they headed back toward the hillock that lay between us and the slope of the meadow which formed the north bank of the pond.

Within five minutes John hit the back door, all ice and annoyance forgotten.

"Maw, you gotta come see. Saint's down on the ice and Daddy says you have to come."

God never yet made a pair of boots that would hold up people like me. I'm one of those who can slip on a perfectly dry floor in the middle of her own kitchen and Sam knows it. To send John to get me was incredible.

"She's splayed out right smack in the middle of the ice with her back legs straight out behind and her front legs out to the sides!"

"That's not possible!"

"Wait'll you see her!"

I put on the biggest pair of boots I could find in the stack by the back door. (*Why is there never a pair that fits*, I wondered irritably.) Telling Becca to stay put and answer the phone, I headed out with John. We made it down the steps (there's a rail there) and across the yard. By the time we had reached the top of the hillock, however, I had tumbled three times. There was no way I was ever going to make it over the terracing and down to Sam. Quickly, John ran back up the slope to the fence where Sam and Becca had propped her sled the day before. I got on and he pulled. All he said was "Honestly!" but I thought it covered most of the bases for both of us.

Just as he crested the last terrace with me and the sled in tow, he lost control, tumbled, and the sled and I went racing down the sloping pasture straight for the pond. I came to an alarming halt just at the edge of the ice and looked smack into the faces of an incapacitated Saint and a startled husband who had barely managed to jump clear in time. Saint and I viewed each other from our relative positions of indignity, and I couldn't decide who was the more pitiable. While John muttered "Honestly!" once more

41

from behind me and while young Sam wisely began to kick at the mounds of snow, Sam, Sr. pulled me off the grounded sled. Despite the fact that his "one cow up and one to go" has continued to be a bit of a sore point between us in the months since, there was something to be said for the accuracy of his summation.

Certainly, getting Saint up was not going to be so easy. For one thing, Saint didn't have a sense of humor. In fact, looking at her mournful eyes as she lay helpless on the ice, I realized she didn't have much hope either, or much time. Sam had become sober, too.

"She's getting sleepy already," he said. And indeed her eyes were closing more frequently and staying closed longer. Hypothermia.

There was no way to get either the pickup or the tractor across the icy fields and down to her. Even assuming we could get the machinery to her, there would be no traction for them to pull her weight by.

Leaving me with her—for how they ever proposed to get me out of there was still unresolved—the men went back toward the barn for rope and the hand crank. In all the years that Saint and I had shared these fields, I had never liked that cow and the feeling was mutual. She was horned and huge, so majestic with all that headgear that Sam had refused to dehorn her. The result was that she was queen of the feeding bins. What Saint wanted, Saint always got, even from me. More than once I had worn on my skin a blue circle of bruise where Miss Saint had reminded me that she was capable of enforcing her will. Now she lay before me dying, and for the first time I was grateful for the horns. They were our one hope.

Sam came back over the hill with the rope, an iron

stake, and the hand crank. Lassoing her horns, he cinched the rope around that magnificent crown, drove the stake into the frozen bank, and began cranking. After ten minutes, he had moved her only a few inches. He sent John and Sam, Jr. out onto the ice to push as he pulled. They both fell flat every time Saint slid even a hair's width closer to the bank, but the scheme was working.

"Talk to her. Make noise," Sam snapped at me.

I talked. Lord knows what I said, but I talked, and she opened her eyes and closed them and opened them and dozed again.

"Damned cow. Too stupid to see where the edge is. Bet she loses that calf!"

He cranked, the boys shoved, I talked. In time, probably less than an hour actually, we had her over to the bank, but still on the ice. Sam and the boys went to the barn for hay. They came back tumbling and slipping, but each boy had a bale and Sam had two. They broke the bales open and covered her completely. Sam sent John back for the camp stoves and set two of them to burning on the bank near her head.

We had done all we could do. There was no way to crank her up onto the bank itself. Once we had the bulk of her off the slippery surface of the pond, no rope and no man would be strong enough to pull the rest of her over the broken bank and off the frozen water. In distress and despair, Sam shook his head.

"Sure do hate to lose that cow!"

He lifted the rope off her head, patting the spots at the base of her horns where his rope had worn through the hide.

"Come on, boys. Let's get your mother back up that hill."

"Are you just going to leave Saint?"

43

"It's up to her and the hay now. If she's got enough body heat left, the hay will hold it in and warm her up enough for her to move around in about an hour, but I'm sure not going to stand here and watch."

Not stand here and watch her die, I thought silently to myself as I looked at the strain on his face. Roughly he pulled me up and I felt in my shoulder the tug of his anger. He hated unproductive death as only a physician or a farmer can.

It was a tough go back up to the house, but going up hill, as any awkward soul will tell you, is much easier than going down and a whole lot less dangerous. I made the trip back to the fence and the house with no spills and few insults to my self-esteem except for Sam's growling displeasure that I should be so clumsy. We were plainly in for a difficult afternoon.

Womanlike even at nine, Rebecca had sensed that food helps everything, even if it only occupies the anxiety of the cook. She had spent her time wisely. The table was set, a bit crookedly, but set. The teakettle was full and steaming sedately. Cinnamon sticks were on the table and the box of instant hot chocolate was set out beside five unmatched mugs. *Not bad,* I thought to myself. *There's hope for this child yet.* And she was right, of course. The men threw down gloves and scarves and sat, still in their dungarees, drinking instant chocolate while I got out sandwich makings. Some Sunday lunch! Some ending to Advent!

Sam's mood mellowed with the warmth and the food and the removal to happier company. But by one o'clock he was fidgeting again.

"Come on, boys. And bring the ax."

This time they left me behind, but as soon as they were safely gone, Rebecca began to beg to go just as far as the back fence. That I could probably do safely and I, too, found the inside intolerable. I threw the remains of lunch into the refrigerator and the dishes into the sink and out we went.

The boys were already standing at the pond by the time she and I got to the hillock. We grabbed her sled and this time we both used it as a seat from which to watch the scene below us. Sam was over beyond the pond near the windbreak chopping down a rather sizable young sapling.

"What's he going to do?" she queried.

I thought I knew, but I wasn't sure.

"Watch him."

He brought the sapling down with another blow and picked it up in both hands as if testing its weight. Then he swung it a time or two, nodding his head as if in approval. Picking up the ax, he headed back toward the boys and the pond. Beyond him Saint lay still as death.

He must have spoken to the boys because they both moved back. He set the ax down and as suddenly as a thought comes, he began to beat the cow with the tree. Hard. Harder. Blow after blow ringing across the winter fields as flesh broke beneath his fury.

"No, Daddy, No!"

Rebecca was suddenly on her feet and about to run when I grabbed her and pulled her back. The tears were already in her eyes as she fell back into my lap and buried her face in my chest. She sobbed as the blows continued to ring out.

"He's killing her! He's going to kill her!"

Then the blows stopped.

"Look," I told her quietly.

Peeking out from my neck she looked. Saint, however briefly, had risen with the last blow, staggered for an instant and fallen forward. Down again, but this time safely down on the bank. She was exhausted, but she was off the ice. Through her tears Rebecca watched with me as the boys scooped the hay back up off the ice, re-covered her in her new position on the snow and reset the stoves. The men headed back up toward us, Sam leaving the sapling beside the fallen cow and bringing the ax with him as he came. Up the hill and still looking grim he came.

"Not out of the woods yet," he mumbled at me as he passed us.

This time he went in, dropped his winter clothes at the back door, and went straight upstairs to our bedroom where he settled into his recliner and was instantly asleep.

The wind dropped a bit and the snow stopped. Near midafternoon I called Sam, Jr. to come feed the stock and John to go break open his water hole. Roused by my voice, Sam came down and with only "I'll be back" was into his clothes and out the door again. This time I did not go to watch but even in the house I could hear the thwacks as the blows fell. Rebecca cringed and covered her ears, looking fearfully up at me only once just before the noise ceased.

John came in first.

"He's got her half way to the barn this time. You got any more stove fuel? One's burned out."

"I gave it to him and went on peeling the vegetables to put in with the pot roast. Heavy fare. We would need that too by nightfall. The back door opened and shut; Sam walked in and dropped into his chair.

"Got anymore of that chocolate, Princess?"

Not a word about the cow, but still not too tired to remember how much a little girl needs to help. Before

the chocolate was finished, Sam was dozing again and we let him sleep.

Five o'clock came and time for the weekend news. I turned it on to a thirty minute recitation of storm news and thought sardonically that no city newscaster had any idea what a storm really means. Hearing the television, Sam roused.

"Time to go try again," he mumbled as he struggled back into his boots one more time.

Rebecca didn't cry this time or even cringe, despite the fact that the blows were nearer and therefore louder. John heard them also and quietly went out to help, Sam, Jr. trailing behind him a few minutes later.

By seven-thirty I realized that I hadn't heard any blows for quite a while. I looked out. The barn lights were on and I could see shadows moving. They had got her in! Sure enough, before I had reheated the vegetables, Sam, Jr. came in grinning.

"Daddy says get supper ready. We're starving!"

Within fifteen minutes we were all sitting down and ravenous. Sam, the last to come in, had not even bothered to take off his overalls. Too hungry to wait, he had said. And that peculiar pungency which comes from manure as it thaws began to fill the kitchen pleasantly as we started to pass our plates.

"Daddy has to light his candle first," Rebecca chimed just as we were ready to eat at last. "It's Joseph's Sunday," she insisted and went to get the matches.

"Well, he sure smells like Joseph."

John has always muttered his wry comments under his breath, but this one got heard. Suddenly, the afternoon's tension was broken, and we all started laughing until the tears rolled down our cheeks. As Sam rose above our laughter to light the father's candle in the wreath on the table, Rebecca grabbed him hard around the waist and hugged him.

He may smell like Joseph, I thought to myself amidst their laughter, *but we will never know if Joseph were ever loved even half so much.*

The purple candle flickered and caught. The Advent circle on our table was at last complete.

December 21

The only apostle to be remembered and called to mind during the days of late Advent and Christmas is St. Thomas the Doubter, who was also called "Didymus." It is in heritage that many of us first see Our Lord and in ritual that we continue to understand what we cannot speak. Thomas knew that ground well, knew what it was to flounder in confusion, to be asked to follow what had not yet been perceived. He has, thereby, become a kind of symbol himself, a precursor for us who, in four days, will enter into the sanctuary of simpleness and be asked to believe the impossible.

Those of us who come forth into the Epiphany believing will be, as was Thomas himself, people of passion—"converted," to use the rhetoric of the church. As a result, St. Thomas' Day is the somberest one in the church's year save for Good Friday itself, to which it is a near analog.

5

THE DAYS OF DIDYMUS

I've never been one of those who can anticipate Christmas unhesitatingly and with impunity. It's one of those anxieties that I wish I could cover up or hide, the kind that causes one as much shame as discomfort.

The children—at least our children—begin in early September, before the first whiff of fall air cools the meadow, to sing carols and folk songs. In fact, after every Labor Day, they do a kind of musical lunge forward, completely jumping Halloween and Thanksgiving and going straight for the jackpot.

In those weeks of September when the singing first begins, I feel their enthusiasm. There is a heady ten days in there when I think that this time it's going to be different. I have even been known over the years, especially in our milder Septembers, to sit down a night or two at the piano in the front hall and stroke out my rendition of "Silent Night," the only thing I still retain from years of piano lessons.

And, with all seriousness, I know deep inside my own meditative parts that I really do want it to be different this year, that I would like the confusion to be fun for them and us, and for the interruption of routine to be pleasurable for just one December in our lives. But then Halloween gives way to Thanksgiving which inevitably gives way to Advent and suddenly it's St. Thomas' Day and we are into it again!

I don't mean the commercialization of Christmas. Obviously Christmas is a cultural phenomenon as well as a religious event, even in the country, and as such is of course commercialized. But Easter is commercialized too, not only by its bunnies and baskets, but also by its emphasis on new clothes and parades. Yet Easter fits. It fits the rotations of the earth, the budding of the trees, the lengthening of the days, the raucousness of the birds and animals mating in every tree and pasture. Easter is rebirth so completely and so universally that one does not have to work at believing it or labor to celebrate it. God makes Easter and all creation enjoys it. People make Christmas.

At our house where both Daddy and his offspring love to bake in the evenings, the holiday cooking is hardly an extra or a problem. While the decorating is not a favorite activity, we have learned to accomplish it early in Advent when the routine of school and work still hold and when decorating is still more pleasant than the alternatives of homework or deskwork.

But the gift-buying is another matter entirely. By simple logic (I'm the one who enjoys the greatest flexibility during the daylight hours when most shopping can be done), the job of buying and wrapping the gifts falls to me.

My discomfort with the gifts is a result of the contradictions that render me impotent to deal with buying them. By the very nature of things, there is a limit

to the time that can be expended in acquiring them
and an even greater limit to the money that can be
spent. While the season's moralizers will always
claim that the amount spent is not important ("It's the
thought that counts"), intelligence and simple obser-
vation militate strongly against that position. The
thought behind a standard boy's bike and the feel of a
ten-speed racer under that same boy are very, very
unequal to a fourteen-year-old. They are also very unequal to my checkbook.

The inequality and the loss of time grow when they
are multiplied by seven children, children-in-law,
grandchildren, grandmothers, and godparents. The
real issue here, however, is that children need to experience the security and the largess of having those
this-world things that help them fit easily into the pat-
terns and flow of their own lives, both social and domestic, private and public. For fourteen-year-olds in a
farming village that means ten-speed racers, and it
means, if we are to walk in balance in January, less for
someone else.

How about an older sister? Maybe cut a corner
there. She's married now, just starting a home, making contacts and friends, wanting to entertain, going
out as a young-married, getting off to a good career
start, finding that two salaries don't cover it all in the
beginning. She would love the food processor, has
asked for one, in fact, and can remember that when
one asked at fourteen for the reasonable (and especially when one could explain one's reasonableness),
one got the item usually. And, she has explained, it
not only would make meals easier for them, but it
would make possible the fancier hors d' oeuvres and
dishes that friends are learning to prepare for each
other. Good training for being grown-up some day. It

also lies outside the budget if the racer is to show up. Multiplying these dilemmas and the hours it takes to wrestle with them by fifteen or twenty people reduces me to an inertia that is almost paralyzing.

By St. Thomas' Day, I have obviously lost all sense of stables and stars. But more insidious, more dark than that, I have lost my sense of why. It is into the fields and down to the pond that I always take my weariness and my doubt, in the process and flow of the system that I find steadiness. But in late December the pond is frozen, all its life sealed below my view and my sharing. The animals stand huddled in the barn or against the windbreaks, too cold to come for their treat of cottonseed meal. Even Percy the cat won't walk the fields with me. Alone in the cold at pond's edge in that deep death, only solitude seems good, and sleep becomes the greatest gift.

Yet at the top of the hill and through the fence still wait the house, the children, the holiday I cannot escape. I doubt the worth of all my efforts as well as my pain, doubt the rightness of even trying to bring birth day and celebration to so much stasis.

"Lord, we know not whither thou goest; and how can we know the way?" (John 14:5) I always thought it wonderfully appropriate that St. Thomas should have asked that question before Calvary. As I stand at the pond, staring at the opaque ice, I take it as my question.

Gifting is a way to demonstrate love. It requires that we study another so intensely as to perceive his or her unspoken desires and meet them. It means to startle with the unexpected, perfectly chosen. For our children we have always seen it as a way to form a thankful and satisfied adult, to create a readiness for generosity, the early habits of appreciation, and a sense of blessedness.

But already I am defeated, for I can accomplish only so much of this and no more. I go back up the hill and through the fence into the yard sure that this Christmas I'll make a wrong selection, disappoint one of the children beyond the limits of his or her vulnerability, lose God's voice as I have lost God's creatures, be too weary to worship.

All of which is to say that there is immeasurable risk involved in Christmas, whether the popular pulpit wants to admit it or not. In many ways I suspect, like St. Thomas, that the days from the Joseph candle to the midnight service on Christmas Eve have very little to do with Jesus or Wise Men or salvation in the minds and attentions of most of us. But they do have a great deal to do with the soul's education.

In all that stress of bearing up under my own limitations and of exposing my failures to those I love; in all that searching to understand the next name on the list well enough to buy something that will be reasonably near where he or she really is in life; in all that yearning to continue creating good things inside our children, knowing the process has grown beyond my reach—in all that, there is not only the sense of doubt and impotence but also there is always the sense of release that comes at ten o'clock on Christmas Eve.

At our house nowadays, the gifts are opened by then. In earlier days they weren't opened until Christmas, but the effect is the same. Going out the door toward midnight service I always, invariably and blessedly, feel that relaxation which says it is done, that this one event in which we integrate and inter-react with each other more intensely than at any other time has reached its climax. Tomorrow we can go back to living together again, each of us as ourselves, and quit for another year trying to project into each other's wants and needs and desires. We can go back to the simple knowledge that in giving and receiving we have been involved at the deepest level of intimacy, have failed in places and succeeded in others. We have stopped to know each other in the stillness of the winter with no help outside ourselves, no impetus, no motivation beyond our own will to make holy the day for our God.

It has always seemed to me worth remembering that Christmas, while it is the high festival of the church, is also the only holy day we routinely celebrate in the dark of the night. And that the good man honored in those harsh days from the Joseph candle to the midnight mass is indeed St. Thomas the Doubter, old Didymus himself. I have long suspected the ancient church fathers who assigned functions and places in the liturgical calendar of a deep, if somewhat wry, wisdom. Certainly every year in the middle of that service when the Host is elevated and the first "Hosanna" rises from the choir loft, I can say with Thomas, "My Lord and my God!" (John 20:28) And each year that has made all the difference.

Christmas Eve

In no other part of the holy season do religious customs and family traditions so vary, or the world so intrude into the truth of things, as in the forty-eight hours of December 24 and 25. Perhaps the incarnation happens not only with the coming of the Child, but also, in some limited fashion, with every activity of his birth day.

It may be that in anthems and carols, bread and wine, sermon and scripture we touch the stuff of God. It is also surely true that in feast and family custom, excess and poignancy, sentimentality and food baskets we touch the best of ordinary humanity. Only at Christmas do religious custom and family tradition run side by side, overlapping and intertwining and blending into that childlike abandon which we, at any other time of year, associate with saintliness and mysticism.

When we actually celebrate the religious observances (or perhaps whether we even do so or not) seems to me to matter less on December 24 and 25 than at any other time of the liturgical year, for somehow the season itself redeems even the worst of us. It is as if life cannot bear for this one time of the year to be desecrated and arranges purification through community, however briefly, for all of us.

6

CHRISTMAS EVE GIFT

It seems to me, in looking back over my fifty-odd years, that pecans have always been something of an issue in my wintertimes.

Sam comes from six generations of mountain stock who have always garnered their supplies. Mountaineer reasoning about frugality is basically defensible. Appalachians conserve everything in order to survive a geography that has no intention of allowing them or anything else nonvegetative to survive. Also, of course, there are no pecans indigenous to Appalachia. It is a remembered omission which, even now, years after our having left the mountains, makes the nuts of disproportionate importance to Sam, or so I always thought until recently.

My folks, by contrast, were second and third generation West Tennessee. While as a climate the Mississippi Valley leaves a great deal to be desired in terms of human comfort, it certainly does know how to produce good pecans as well as good cotton and soy beans. So, although I grew up as a transplant from West Tennessee into Appalachia, I never wanted for pecans. In fact, every relative we had left behind along the Mississippi (and my father alone had fifteen brothers and sisters, which will give you a notion of the nut glut to which I refer here), every cousin, sibling, and in-law along the River sent us a shoe box of pecans sometime between Thanksgiving and Mother's Christmas cooking.

The fact that the nuts always arrived in shoe boxes seemed perfectly natural to me as a child, as did the fact that the nuts were already nicely cracked. Little spots of grease would always have seeped through the heavy cardboard in transit, leaving dark circles along the sides and bottoms of the boxes and making the cotton cords around them turn faintly brown and wonderfully aromatic.

It was always a matter of great urgency to my mother that the nuts be transferred immediately to mason jars and sealed tightly against any further insults to their freshness. I secretly suspected that she would have been happier if each relation had presented his or her gift in person, that traveling the four hundred miles between the River and the mountains would have been, in her mind, a small price to pay for something so precious as absolute freshness in the Christmas nuts.

Those nuts suspected of being less than perfect were set aside for roasting. (Sister Mattie was a spinster and therefore had no husband to give proper pruning and fertilizer to the trees, while Brother Murph was married but childless and took great pride in giving detailed attention to his trees, and so on and so forth.) In the evenings of early December, as the nut boxes began to accumulate on the kitchen counter, my father roasted the pecans on trays in the old Majestic oven, allowing the nuts to arrive just at the peak of mahogany which marks a good nut. Those meats incapable of perfection of color he set off in a bowl and shared the next day with the squirrel family which, to his great satisfaction, came winter after winter to live in our mailbox. They loved the goodies which kept them there, and the postal system in those days was better-natured than in our times. So our mail froze, the squirrels ate without storing up for winter, and no nut was wasted. Mountain frugality was contagious even among non-natives.

The nuts that were known to be superb (Murph's, in particular, and Ryce's sometimes, but only after tasting the box liberally for this year's quality), the nuts that were of sufficient oil content, color, and texture had to be sorted into the perfect halves and the broken pieces and, lastly, of course, into the goodies.

It was my job to sort. Hour after hour I sat at the kitchen table sorting the boxes my mother had set before me as being worthy of her kitchen as they were. The big halves she jarred for decorating the pecan pies. There would be about three dozen sent out as gifts before Christmas. The medium-sized halves she jarred for decorating the fruit cakes (never more than ten of those) and the steamed bread (never enough of that ever!) The little halves she jarred for the dearth that inevitably would come in the spring when any nut would look good in her Waldorf salads. By custom, they took their place in the refrigerator where the whole bottom shelf would be full of nut jars until at least July.

The big, broken pieces were the ones with which I exercised the greatest care. They went into the divinity, which I didn't like, and the fudge, which I adored. Any child who has ever bitten into absolutely succulent fudge only to hit a sliver of pecan shell knows immediately the motivation behind my carefulness. Checking the big pieces for shell was the only domestic chore, in fact, that I ever felt any sense of quality about as a child. I checked those nuts until my fingers were brown and the tips sore almost to bleeding. My pecans were perfect, shell-less, and guaranteed not to be bitter.

The smaller pieces went into my mother's fudge cake, widely regarded as the apex of area cooking. She shared her recipe with any and every one who asked for it, but she never shared her pecans or her highly trained staff—us—for the preparation of the major ingredient. The result was that Christmas began with the fudge cake at Mrs. Alexander's tea.

The open house ("tea" was the more elegant name my mother preferred, but it was also a totally absent part of the menu) was always held on December 20 and 21 in the afternoons from three until seven o'clock and involved upwards of four hundred souls: the faculty, staff, and internationals from the university where my father was the dean; the ladies (with their husbands) of the Monday Club, the Dilettantes, the church circle, the Thursday Bridge Club; and the neighbors, of course, since they could hardly avoid perceiving that "The Tea" was happening again at the Alexanders.

At those Christmas teas, it was a mark of dear friendship and high standing when one left by way of the kitchen door, a plate of extra pieces of fudge cake having been sent home to the children. I always suspected the children never saw much of the result of that honor.

The nut goodies were, by contrast, the bane of my existence. They were, I remember telling Mama tearfully, too pesky to be worth it. The tiny little bits of nut were so oily that all the shell dust stuck to them, brown like shell bits and almost indistinguishable from those bitter enemies in the weak light of the kitchen, too small to ever fill up a cup measure much less a mason jar.

Everything was wrong with the goodies, except the nut balls Mother made from them. Night after night I would separate out goodies and night after night she and my father would convert the bits into cookie sheets full of balls about the size of small jaw-breakers. I never knew what held the nuts together, but I knew the result. Once the balls had seasoned for a week in the open air, they were carefully rolled in confectioner's sugar and stored in waxed paper in tins. I could never decide which was worse, the cookie sheets over every surface in the kitchen and pantry and breakfast room or the dozens of tins that had to be fetched out of storage, cleaned, filled, and then stacked up every wall and in every corner of the kitchen, pantry, and breakfast room.

There was a time, of course, as there is for all of us, when I enjoyed the long evenings in the kitchen, the camaraderie of shared chores, the anticipation of how effusively the party would be praised, the home-cooked gifts received, the Christmas feast enjoyed. That time fell within those sleeping years when I assumed it was so in every household, for I had no experience outside that household, no basis for knowing of other ways and other habits. As with all innocence, so with mine.

In adolescence I came to resent the ache in my shoulders, the three weeks of stain on my hands, the interruption of my evenings, the disturbance of tins and mason jars and cookie sheets everywhere in my space. In time I came to see with the wisdom of wider experience that *the* party was dedicated to my father's career and my mother's domestic prowess, not to Christmas; that the holiday was only an excuse which made the inevitable less obviously self-serving. My increasing awareness of the holiness of the season made our social tour de force more and more repugnant to me. By the time I was twenty, the teas had stopped and I was devout and free of Christmas as well as of pecans.

When I was twenty-one, Sam and I married and moved to West Tennessee. During those early years of medical school, general practice, residency, specialization, fellowships, and babies, I resisted both Christmas and pecans which were its symbol. There were no hours for sitting around kitchen tables sorting and cleaning nut pieces and certainly no energy for cooking quantities and quantities of frill foods. With seven children I did well to get supper on the table, much less put feasts there. Besides, we lived in the city and had no pecan trees in our yard, and for one reared as a connoisseur, store-bought pecans are worse than no pecans at all! So for twenty years I avoided the whole issue of the Christmas nuts and, thereby, most of middle-class, American Christmas itself—beyond the necessity of Santa Claus, of course.

Then we moved to the country. We had bought the farm and signed the papers before I found it—the prettiest Stewart tree I ever saw, perfect in shape, full, and not fifty feet from its mate, which I had also somehow failed to see. We were back into the pecan business. My heart sank.

Sure enough, on the afternoon of our first Thanksgiving in the country, frugality resurfaced. Sam announced to the two boys that they were to get out the empty feed sacks and come gather nuts. He got the familiar long pole of West Tennessee farmers and began the knocking and rattling of the tree limbs. Both trees kindly rendered up sack after sack of nuts, and sack after sack of nuts came in my kitchen door, this time still in the husks even! I was definitely back in the nut business.

During the nights of that first Christmas, we sat in the kitchen and sorted. The husks were sacked back into the shed in order to be put around the azaleas in the spring. The shells were likewise sacked and stored for the rose beds. "Waste not, want not," I could remember Sam's mother saying over and over again through the years.

The best nuts were lovingly sorted out, sacked in Baggies and packaged for mailing to the oldest girl who had already married and moved away. Shades of my own childhood! I could suddenly see my grandson with brown fingers and sore shoulders sorting our nuts in another kitchen, more modern but no better lit than that of my own childhood. *Poor baby,* I thought, *I'm so sorry to do this to you.*

The remaining nuts were sorted by three pairs of adolescent hands into halves for pies, chunks for candy, and goodies for the squirrels. (I had a sense of *déjà vu* many times during that first winter back on the farm.)

Then, in the spring, Sam set out the cuttings, almost two dozen of them, in fact. He tied red yarn around them so that the boys would not run over them with the mower or in their play. From my kitchen window it looked as if all of Lucy, Tennessee, were abloom with red-ribboned Stewart pecans. Year after year he fertilized and grafted and tended, and the papershells thrived, and we garnered—until last year.

It was the hard spring freeze that did it, everyone said. I don't know enough about pecans to gauge the accuracy of that explanation, but I do know that there were no pecans. The trees never bloomed, never tasseled, never made nuts. There were no long evenings in the kitchen in early December, no brown fingers, no aching shoulders. Instead, we took out of the freezer the nuts we had put back the year before. We made candies and fruitcake and baked the nut pies for Christmas dinner, and I gave the whole thing no thought beyond a vague sense of relief until three days before Christmas when the twelve-year-old remarked morosely, "I missed the pecans this year."

"Whatever for? We have a freezer full!"

"I missed the doing them," and he walked out the door to do his evening chores in the hen house.

I looked at Sam and he looked at me. The next afternoon he came home from town with three big sacks full of the worst looking, unshelled pecans I have ever seen. Where he managed to beg or buy them he never said and I never asked, but we all sat down—the five of us still at home—and interrupted our lives to let the nuts in.

We cracked, shelled, and sorted nuts we didn't need for dishes we wouldn't eat and sacked more for a freezer that couldn't hold them. We baked one more fudge cake and roasted nuts for the nursing stations at the hospital (which made Sam a huge hit the next day, I was told later). We dulled my kitchen floor (already waxed for the holiday) with nut dust, cluttered every countertop with bowls and jars, and dirtied every cookie sheet we own. And when it was done, when we had finally finished the last nut, we laughed and drank eggnog from the back porch crock and sang silly songs by candlelight (so none of us could see the mess we had made). And we—all five of us—went to bed mightily content.

Sometime during the night I woke, went downstairs to my destroyed kitchen, and sampled a piece of fudge cake. Standing in the square of windowed moonlight, I pondered philosophically just how it was that in the pursuit of the valid and religious I had somehow, over the years, failed to understand the value of the secular and human, had missed seeing that the one always serves the other. I was peaceful in my new wisdom. The fudge cake in my mouth was still faintly warm and rich . . . until I bit down on the nuts. Then I laughed. Standing alone in my kitchen at two o'clock on Christmas Eve morning, I laughed. The pecans were stale! Mealy! Bitter to my tongue! But they were sweet as Christmas itself to my heart.

December 26

In moving from the Old World to the New, the church suffered certain insults to its calendar as well as to its liturgy, none of them being more buried in origin or more mourned in song than St. Stephen's Day. Were it not, in fact, for the children who carol "Good King Wenceslas" with such gusto for half of every winter, we would probably have lost the good saint completely at our house.

As things stand, he still remains among us, I fear, as a diffuse image of mixed background, a happy confusion of the handsome young man who died triumphantly in the heat and sand outside Jerusalem and the stooped, fur-wrapped parade of king, servant, and serf trudging for all time through the deep recesses of some Nordic forest. The sense of celebration and rejoicing over martyrdom is about as far removed from American experience as is that Nordic forest. And I for one would certainly be among the first to question its desirability, if not its utility.

Yet the song persists around here, and with it the questions of the children. At first, "Who was St. Stephen?" Then, as they mature, "Why St. Stephen at Christmas?" Because what we get up with on December 26 is what we went to sleep without on December 24, and Stephen was the first human being in recorded history to send us back word of that.

7

SILLY SALLY'S GIFT

It was the first winter since our coming to this place
and the first day after Christmas. We had settled into
that most tranquil week of the whole year, into those
days that stretch quietly from Christmas to Holy
Name when, as if by common agreement, all of life
stops and rests. The phone rings almost not at all.
Even illness, we have noticed over the years, takes a
rest for the holiday. The mails are light on those days
when they do come, and always social rather than
fiscal—"Dear Uncle Sam and Aunt Phyllis, Thank
you for. . . ." The tins on the counters are still reassuringly full of sweets and the refrigerators, no longer
stressed to the bursting, are nonetheless able to pro-
vide easy meals on demand. I read and doze and indulge the luxury of daydreams while the quarrel-free
children enjoy new toys and each other. Sam goes sel-
dom to the city, his hours in the office and the hospital
both cut to their shortest of the year.

A large open kettle of spiced tea sits on low on the
back eye of the stove all day and all night, the dipper
floating quietly in the auburn spiciness. Even the

dribbles and spots where many hands have filled many mugs inaccurately don't bother me this week. We'll clean it all up the day before school starts and life begins again. The only necessity now is to keep the kettle full and a supply of mugs clean.

Not even neighbors and playmates come. We are too removed to have the former and too many to desire the latter. A godparent or two will make the long haul out to us, share a mug of tea and then, in the shortened daylight, leave early to make his or her way home.

Outdoors the weather was bitter cold that first winter as it has continued always to be after Christmas even in our milder years since. It was the Feast of St. Stephen. By breakfast the first child had already one-fingered "Good King Wenceslas" out of the old *John Thompson's Primer for Beginners* on the piano in the front hall. As I cooked the eggs and warmed the last of the Christmas coffee cakes, I let myself float in the familiar tune and the heady security of repetition. For twenty years some child or other had beat out that tune on the same piano from the same John Thompson while I scrambled eggs and stretched leftover pastries by adroitly cutting them into sufficiency. The younger children have always done it without suggestion or premeditation. That was the miracle, and life was terribly, terribly good as I stood inattentively stirring the eggs.

We sat to eat, Sam in his overalls and flannel shirt, I in my jeans and big woolly, the children variously attired in footed sleepers, pj's, and sweat suits according to their age and relative condition of alertness. We ate and drank and looked for all the world like a Norman Rockwell come to life. I, who have spent a lifetime deploring that fallacious romanticist, cruised easily into being a jeans and flannel-clad part of his reality. Life was indeed good, and one should engage some sentimentality on the Feast of St. Stephen.

The meal over (even adroitness can do only so much), I began to clear the table. The children scattered to dress and to consider how little they could pick up in their rooms without serious consequences. Sam booted up for the barn. He needed to move some more hay down from the loft into the paddocks so the boys could get at it more easily, and the feeding tray for the cottonseed meal needed to be rebraced. I watched him from the kitchen window as he clomped across the yard and down the path between the garden and the orchard, carrying his hands, as he always does, tucked for warmth inside the bib of his overalls. Long before he got to the pasture gate, the herd had heard him and begun moving toward him. By the time he had opened the gate, they were all there waiting to be patted and scratched and slipped a rotten apple or two from the orchard. Before he had re-latched the gate, I lost him in a sea of cows. He reappeared at their head and together the whole mass walked toward the barn.

I finished the cleanup and made our bed, considered being stern about the wrinkled messes which were the other beds and gave it up as not worthy of the season, started to wash and was meditating on some Christmas notes—when I realized Sam had been gone for quite a while. Not a lover of the cold, it's unusual for him to work in the open of December for a couple of hours without coming in to warm up. More to the point, holiday or no holiday, he had to make rounds sometime this morning on the few patients caught in the hospital over the Christmas break. I called John to go check on him and began to assemble my pens and special Christmas notepaper.

I'm a poor letter-writer and make up for it by buying elaborate seasonal stationeries and handsome address books that are kept with various script pens, all of which I take great care in assembling upon the appropriate occasions. The whole process wearies me so that assembling is usually as far as I get. And it was to be so again that first year.

In no time at all (even before I had found the special gold pen I had bought the week before to use on the green paper) John was back in the kitchen door grinning from ear to ear, his cheeks fiery red and the tops of his ears glowing almost as much as his smile. He beat his hands together, his gloves still on, and hollered at me.

"Daddy says get everybody dressed and come quick!"

I hollered back, "Why?" but he was gone as boisterously as he had come, slamming the door behind him.

"Come on, everybody." I stood at that acoustically magic spot in the kitchen from which my voice can go both upstairs to the bedrooms and downstairs to the family room simultaneously.

"Get your coats on quick. Daddy wants us." Then I remembered to add, "Get your gloves too!"

Every room below and above me gave up its supply of Tickles, and every combination of jeans, pj's, flannels, and woolies stopped at the back door to wiggle into boots. We went forth, all of us still struggling with something—a boot, a glove, a pajama leg still caught halfway up a jeans leg—but we went forth.

As we made it into the pasture and halfway to the barn, we saw John's head cresting the hillock that blocked our view of the close below. As John topped

the rising, Sam emerged, head first, behind him. And on his shoulders, wrapped around the back of his neck and held there by his gloveless hands, he carried something. The smile on his face was greater even than John's, and he came across the hillock crest with a spring in his gait that I hadn't seen there in years.

The children stopped where they were and Mary, eighteen and home from college, whispered, "It's a calf!"

That was all it took. The troops broke and ran toward Sam, following him like a swarm of dancing dervishes as he led his triumphant procession into the barn. The stall was instantly a center of warmth and activity as a dozen hands tried to touch and stroke. Behind us I could hear Silly Sally bawling up the hillock (it was, after all, *her* calf), making her way toward the barn. The children shouted and shoved and giggled passionately as the calf struggled to her feet and, seeing us, bawled her first cry for her mama. They were enchanted and totally forgetful of us when Sam turned to me, the grin still filling his face.

"We've made it," he said.

"We've made it," I answered and left.

The land had borne well for us that first summer. Our cupboards were full of mason jars of beans and beets and peaches, the bins with potatoes, onions, and even pears and green tomatoes, the freezer with fruit and squash and corn. But this was our first calf. Our herd had reproduced and the result was life.

I rounded the barn and got to the garden side of it before I began to cry. As soon as I had managed to swipe away some of my tears with my sleeve and quiet some of my heaving by holding onto the barn, I watched as they came out. Mary first, a Kleenex held

73

defiantly to her face. Laura next, running for the house. Even John, quiet as he never is, slipping around to the other side of the hay feeder to make a great show of loving Silly Sally by burying his face in her side. The two Sams eventually came out and Rebecca with them, riding the way the calf had done, astraddle her father's shoulders. And they came singing, Sam's rich baritone breaking over the meadows, "Good King Wenceslas looked out, on the Feast of Stephen. . . ."

Before the day was done, Philip would drive out from town for dinner and we would call Nora in Knoxville with the news. We would also call every schoolmate we could think of and the whole miracle would be told again and again to people who really probably don't yet understand why a calf was so important, so singular, an occurrence.

When the children had all finally gone off to their beds, I settled into a warn tub, drawing the day and the comfort around me. In a big family a new baby gets to be so ordinary, especially for the older children who have seen it time and again and who know what it means in lost sleep and increased work. They may joke about swelling bellies and pregnant mamas, but they have no anxiety beyond dreading the first year with another infant sibling—and they certainly have no sense of wonder. "The youngest of us is two. Of course Mother is pregnant. What else is new?"

Somehow I hadn't realized over the years that the meaning of Christmas had diminished for them as a result, that the joy everyone else spoke of and reported and sent us greeting cards about had become incomprehensible to all of us from sheer habit. Soaking in the tub, I understood that Silly Sally had given the joy of birth back to us.

As I crawled into bed, I poked Sam to wake him. "Merry Christmas," I said as he grinned and took me in.

December 27

St. John the Evangelist was the celebrant of Christianity as a religion rather than a spokesman for it as an historical event. And someday, if we are ever alone together (outside the pages of a book, of course, where my words won't be caught forever and where neither priest nor episcopate can charge heresy), I'll tell you why I think poets speak more truth with their metaphors than pastors ever do with their dicta. Suffice it here—caught as we are in public view and in immutability—for me to say that I am persuaded, increasingly as I grow older, that the symbol, which may begin as a way of teaching by image what cannot be effectively conveyed as fact, ends up in maturity as the truth it symbolized.

St. John knew things and found them to be of the essence of the Christ. Quite naturally he also found them to be nothing other than the truth; and because of that, he, alone perhaps of all the apostles, understood incarnation. Of course Christ loved him best. How could it have been otherwise between them?

8

DOWN IT COMES

Of all the pleasures of Christmas there is none greater than the taking down and the putting away. In our house it's always done on St. John's Day, the decision having been a kind of long-standing compromise between my desire to get things back to order and the children's desire to avoid all order as long as possible.

It is a contention as old as mothers and children, I suspect; but it is eased at our house by the fact that Sam, who loves disorder better than rare steak, also is deathly allergic to pine, cedar, mistletoe, balsam, holly, haw bush, and so forth. Everything you can think of to decorate with triggers his whole respiratory mechanism into one mass of protest. This phenomenon puts half of him in the children's camp and a much more visible half in Mother's camp. The sooner the order comes, the sooner the gasping stops.

I have always been too grateful for his asthmatic tendencies to be properly regretful of the discomfort they produce, I fear. When we have made it to St.

John's Day and the troops are protesting the breaking down of Christmas too vociferously, I am assured that one fairly emphatic roar from Sam will accomplish for me what further hours of wheedling might, with luck, eventually get done. By midmorning on St. John's Day, therefore, the boxes are almost always down from the attic and strewn across the hall, the living room, and all of the kitchen.

By common agreement, gifts are first carried into each bedroom. The result, of course, is a diffusion of the confusion which had hitherto been somewhat contained in the familyroom. The sight of six beds buried under chaos always makes me hesitant to proceed. At least yesterday I could shut the den doors and not look. But when I waffle, Sam roars and we return to the business at hand.

The agenda, established over the years, calls for continued dissemination. Once the gifts are sorted, the goodies have to be sorted.

There is no chore in all of Christmas like the division of the candy, fruit, and nuts. Over the three days of total carnival everyone has shared sweets and treasures with everyone. Now suddenly, in picking them all up into piles, the discovery comes that over half of each one's store is gone. The fact that each has gained five pounds in three days never seems to translate into any sense of personal consumption. The conclusions are loudly asserted, even by the older children.

"John stole my caramels!"

"Sam ate all the peppermints!"

"Devie copped the Brazil nuts!" (etc.)

One year Sam, Sr. was viciously accused of having done away with all the chocolate covered cherries. It was a charge I subjectively found to be very probable in view of his fondness for them, but I never said so. I strangle on them myself so I was immune to criticism, but they did catch me one year on the tangerines. I denied the allegation, of course, but I spent a lot of St. John's Day in the bathroom and my pleas of innocence suffered in the public assessment as a result.

Nonetheless, the goodies have to be reallocated, however paltry their number and condition seventy-two hours after Christmas. All my kitchen bowls, the ones I have just gotten back from weeks of cooking and returned clean to my now normal cupboards, are assigned, a bowl to a customer, filled with the treasures of each, tagged by their owners, and set on the kitchen counters. The resulting warfare which will surround the bowls for the next week is a bit like the current situation in the Middle East and I always dread it. Arbitrating Hershey's kisses for five-year-olds is one thing, but it's darned silly when it's between a fourteen-year-old and a nineteen-year-old, a point I keep making each year to an absolutely deaf audience.

Once the goodies are into arbitration, the papers and trash go next. Somehow that is the turning point for me every year. Once the trash collecting begins, I feel a wondrous sense of hope. Rebecca, because she is the youngest, fetches the plastic sacks which she begins to fill. An older youngster precedes her, picking the warranties, registration cards, and instructions out of the litter ahead of her. The great mystery of the process annually is that the warranty kid will each year find at least one set of instructions for something no one got or a registration for something that was broken two days earlier. It's the ironies of life that make holidays possible anyway, so why not their aftermath as well?

Once the imported and newly acquired mess is dispensed with, we turn to refilling the boxes with the decorations. It's almost always necessary to eat before the decorations are actually attacked, however, the stress of the warranties having wiped all of us out.

After a meal (which always occurs without regard to the time of day, so I can't say after lunch or supper), we begin the decorations. The lights first, each year accompanied by my protests that we should really throw away the dead bulbs while we still know which ones they are and leave only the new ones, countered by insistence that that's a waste of effort. We'll do it next year when we get them out; we never do, of course. Then the balls and figures and ornaments, each wrapped lovingly in tissue and set carefully in the segmented cartons. The pace slows down as the little creatures are wrapped away. The ball that just won't make it another year, the hole in its side grown too big to hide anymore—"But I remember when I bought it at the Santa Claus Fair when I was five!" The angel that has to be repaired—"Remember, I made her for you when I was in first grade?" The gilded macaroni that each year sheds a few more shells and each year is carefully folded into its tissue because "we strung it the year we came here and got the gold paint all over the patio. Remember? Man, was Daddy mad!"

John, who does the hauling up and down the attic steps, has become quite rigorous with us about throwing away broken and used up decorations. The sentimental side of me has had some trouble with that over the years, since I tend to value still the ornaments that hung on the tree when I was a child or that hung on Sam's tree. (We really did grow up together just like every American boy and girl were supposed to do in the old days before mobility. So I remember his

trees as well as mine and the load up in the attic is thereby twice as great.)

John has figured out how to get around this to some extent by each year sorting out the ancient and useless into boxes which he stuffs farther and farther back into the nether reaches of the attic and which we never see again. The new and consumed he insists on throwing out. "Plastic looks so lifeless in its second year," and out it goes without a fare-thee-well. The sorting is finished and the boxes put back in the attic.

We are suddenly down to the tree itself and the greenery. The greenery is easier and therefore comes first. The boys with cardboard boxes in tow sweep the needles and the branches off the mantels and the bookcases and the tables into the containers and head out to dump them over the pasture fence; then back in for another load. Rebecca and her dust rag come behind them to clear off any resin and dust. One of the older girls replaces the bric-a-brac that has been out of sight in closets and cupboards for the last three weeks; another follows with the vacuum, sucking up the needles that will be with us for months despite her best efforts.

Bit by bit, room by room, the house returns to its normal look of lived-in but collected. I look around at my crew and understand that no one is really sorry. They dread the work and the return to normal—I guess we all do—but it feels good once we get to this stage of things with only the tree left.

The boys begin the job of emptying the washroom. Except for the mop sink, the washer, and the dryer, everything comes out and the door to the yard is propped open. Mary wraps the tree as best she can in an old sheet and they loosen the guy wires that have held it secure these two weeks. They lower it onto the sheet and, picking up sheet and trunk, drag it toward the washroom and the pasture. The cows, already enjoying the earlier greens, are standing at the fence waiting for the tree. By dark they will have managed to demolish most of it. In the next few days one of the boys will bring its stripped frame back in and put it in the chicken yard for the fowl to perch on during the snow months. When the thaws come in March, we will see it there, an icicle or two still twinkling in the spring sunshine.

The last duty of the day is John's. By custom he goes into the kitchen and folds away the Advent wreath, disposing of the candles too burned to save; storing the others, wrapped, in the outside refrigerator for next year; putting the whole in the box marked "Advent" and setting it right at the attic door where he can easily reach it next November. Only the Christ Candle stands, keeping guard over our supper as we sit down to turkey hash and the last of the fruit salad.

It sputters a bit these days, for over the years it has not burned as evenly as it should have and occasionally Sam, Sr. will have to do minor surgery on its walls to keep it going. But everyone gets so nervous when he begins to trim it that his ministrations are kept to a minimum and its sputter to a workable maximum. It first burned at our wedding, a gift from a friend of both families. Now, thirty Christmases and Advents later, it is no longer terribly white or noticeably scented beyond a faint dustiness, but it burns as it has burned every year since our beginning.

The year when the children put it away for the last time will be the year we no longer are here to hold Christmas together, when the holiday will pass to their homes, splitting as it goes from our unity into their new ones. They know that, of course, although we never speak of it, and I think it is why they are so anxious when Sam trims the candle, lest it run out before they are ready to pick up the light for themselves in other candles and other places.

The Christ Candle will burn here each night until the Epiphany when John will make his last trip up to the attic for the long white box with the cellophane top and the blue tissue paper. This too is his ritual. He will take out the ancient blue paper and wrap the candle away, setting it finally beside the Advent wreath just inside the attic and closing the trap door for another year.

Christmas is over, or it will be by bedtime when all the gifts, piled by maternal order on the beds, have of necessity been put away to allow for sleep. The things of the year are absorbed. Most of them were truly appreciated. Some of them earnestly wanted. A few of them such a surprise as to cause the heart joy for years to come. Things are good. All the money that it took, all the saving and arranging and compromising, have been spent for things that lift the spirit and reward the hardness of life, even in the young.

"How dear of him to buy the electric typewriter I wanted and knew we couldn't afford."

"Thank you, Mama!" The squeeze that comes because she has just picked up her first lipstick one last time to put it away and had to find me before she set it permanently on her dresser.

"It's really neat, Dad," as he passes through the kitchen to put the fuel for his new motorized model out in the garage, the model he didn't cut enough grass to buy last summer, despite how hard he tried.

Things! How good they are when they comfort us and reassure us and when they make memories.

How they enrich us, I think, as I blow out the Christ Candle and leave the kitchen.

It has always seemed to me that maybe we bring it all down and sort it all out on St. John's Day more because of St. John than because of Daddy's allergy or my compulsion. We may be the only family in all of Christendom to honor a saint by sorting things, but St. John would bless us, I think. He was the poet of the lot and like all poets he would have understood the lipstick as well as the Christ Candle.

"In the beginning was the Word, and the Word was with God, and the Word was God. The same was in the beginning with God. All things were made by him; and without him was not any thing made that was made. In him was life; and the life was the light of men. And the light shineth in darkness; and the darkness comprehended it not" (John 1:1-5).

"Goodnight, St. John."
"Goodnight, Maw. See ya in the morning!"

January 1

Once a major feast in the church's year, the Holy Name of our Lord Jesus Christ is almost lost for most of us in New Year's Day on which it falls. Holy Name would have us recall that this Child was human and was Jewish; that he was both named and circumcised as an assertion of that humanness. The church bell which tolls at midday across our fields would have us recall that he was also God; it bids us come eat of his flesh, drink of his blood, and enter by name into his unendingness.

9

NAME THIS CHILD

I was seventeen years old when I was first introduced to the psychology of names. Away from home for the first time, I was attending one of those small, southern women's colleges that were long on academic excellence and short on hard cash. The faculty, in those days before equal opportunity legislation, was composed primarily of independently wealthy and brilliantly educated females. One of them was Francesca Boas, daughter of Franz Boas, the father of American anthropology. She fascinated me (and every other undergraduate), and I dogged her heels incessantly.

It must have been October or early November when she laid on me the gem about names. Primitive peoples, she said, even some nonprimitive peoples living in the midst of civilized societies, regard an individual's name as containing the essence of his or her personness. She laid it out before me almost nonchalantly and then watched while a whole system of contradictions and curiosities began to make sense to me: the injunction against taking the Lord's name in vain, the business of christening under a saint's name, the use of Jehovah instead of Yahweh, the giving of titles and surrogates.

Like every other piece of information that explains some part of human experience, I found this one to be enormously satisfying. It should have, in a sense, been like a new toy I could play with until the next tidbit came along to replace it. But there was, in this piece of information, something different. There was an emotional pull, a tugging of the fact at the corners of my feeling as well as of my thinking. This was more than a bauble Francesca had handed me for an afternoon's entertainment. This had to do with something which, though primordial, was still functioning. It had to do with why I wanted to exchange names before I started a conversation, with why first names were different in implication and readiness from surnames and titles, with why General MacArthur was never as good as Ike and why Harry Truman was a better man than both—the sharing of personness. That early freshman wonder never entirely lost its glow, but it subsided eventually, becoming one of those insights that integrated but never was major again until years later when we moved to the country.

A thousand things to name! Like Adam walking into the Garden, the children spent hours naming cats and dogs and cows and chickens. Each new species had to be individually enfranchised as Sam brought it in and added it to the farm's growing population.

Much to our surprise, the whole process was conducted with remarkable care. The new cow that would rather be rubbed and stroked than fed was named, affectionately, Silly Sally. The new Gertrudis with horns was named Saint because she looked like the winged ox which is the icon for St. Luke. The bull was immediately named Bull with a capital "B" since by common agreement he was. By much the same process, Big Mama was christened Big Mama. Nothing else could possibly have covered all her virtues: her broad posterior, her cud-chewing deliberateness, her soft white hide, her gentle, slow eyes and easy affection. She lived out her days with us and annually confirmed the children's accuracy by consistently presenting us with the finest calf of the year.

So we settled in on the Lucy Goosey Farm to share life with Sir Thomas Le Chat, Smokey, Cocoa, Jacon, Junior (he was quite a rooster!), Big Mama, Bull, and company. In time, all of the above tended to reproduce according to the species and place in life assigned to each. Never once was the inventiveness of the children taxed by all of this and, oddly enough I noticed, neither were their memories—or mine or their father's.

Mary was named Mary because she was born to Big Mama on the morning of the day when big sister Mary, much loved and highly valued by the younger children for her unending indulgences, was to come home from college for the spring holiday. Oscar was named Oscar because he had incredibly round ears, walked all his life with a wobble, and looked like an idiot, even for a cow. Beauregard was Molly's calf, and two weeks after calving Molly was the first of the herd to die. But Beauregard was so elegant, so delicate of foot, so careful of his deportment that only the stars knew he was an orphan. Mary (sister, that is) and the younger children bottle-fed him all summer until he could make it alone, but even in that indignity he remained a dandy, demanding that his lip be wiped and his coat stroked clean after each feeding. Only Beauregard would have fit him.

Two years later and in a meadow full of cows, Oscar still was wobbling. He still looked like a bovine idiot the day we penned him up to fatten. For the whole next summer and fall after we had slaughtered, butchered, and frozen him, the children would laugh and giggle at supper. It was always, "Please pass Oscar," instead of "Please pass the meatloaf" or the roast or whatever. The memory of that pathetic dottiness was so pervasive as to even survive metamorphosis.

But in time I began to remark more than the humor in all of this. For instance, Mary grew to be beautiful— not a pretty cow, although she was—but beautiful. Her eyelashes were the thickest I have ever seen on any cow, and her coat was much whiter than her mother's despite the fact that she had been sired by Bull who was black as coal. She was hardly more than a calf herself when she began to indulge the younger children and they even rode her once or twice before I made them stop for her sake. She always got special hay from them and the treats of apples and pears, and even turnips in the later months. It was as if she and they both grew into her name.

It was so also for Beauregard. Long after big sister had gone back to college for another year, he continued his dandy ways. In a herd of three dozen head, you could always spot Beauregard by his gloss as well as by his style. Had a steer been able to swing a fancy stick and wear a top hat, Beauregard would have done both on the day we took him off to market, true as he was to the very end to his name.

It was then that I remembered Francesca again and perceived a corollary to her principle. All things grow into their names, agreed; and all things likewise grow into the names they have given, named and namers reinforcing each other, creating each other for every day of life itself and long beyond the death of the body.

We still see Oscar from time to time in somebody else's dumb steer. The children still "pass Oscar" on nights when the meat is tough, and I am supposed to understand thereby that the cook has failed for at least this meal. And Francesca, herself long since dead, must have smiled last month when the grandson who wasn't even born when Oscar grazed our fields, asked me to please cook him some Oscar for supper.

Mary died this year as gently as she had lived, a calf half-grown within her. The children mourned her as sincerely as if she had been a part of them, for of all the herd, she indeed was knitted to them across all lines and boundaries by a name and by a resulting pattern of life. The other day I listened with a kind of quiet joy as John explained to Rebecca that he was going out beyond Mary's Hill to target practice and she wasn't to follow him. So they have named among themselves the spot where she finally lay down to go.

Tomorrow is the Feast of the Holy Name, the circumcision of Christ, New Year's Day. We will watch our share of American football, of course, and we will go to church as well. But after all of that and before the day is done, I believe I will walk out by myself to Mary's Hill and think there about what it means to know the name of God and to be yourself called by it.

The Epiphany

"Epiphany," when one uses that word, usually means January 6 as a date and the conversion of the Gentiles as an event. It's never been quite that simple in my head. Technically speaking, Epiphany also means the season which stretches from January 6 for six weeks into Septuagesima Sunday and pre-Lent.

In a country where the twelve days of Christmas don't exist any more (except as an impossible song whose final choruses only a genius could remember without a script), Epiphany tends to begin when Christmas as a protected time is over. For folks with our quantity of children, that means the day school reopens. And anyone who thinks that that's not a religious day is just plainly not a mother.

10

THE LAST LITANY

The farm is quiet today: the children back in school, the house sparkling with newfound cleanliness. We spent all of yesterday washing, waxing, and vacuuming, getting them and their rooms ready for the next half of the school year and us and ours ready to turn outward once more to the world beyond the farm and the family. But I am always a thief of this one day. I stay here alone each year, unplug the phones, cut off the lights, and keep holiday alone for one last day before I merge back into life.

Sometimes I write, of course. Sometimes I read. But only rarely do I do either. Mainly I wander from room to room, looking out of windows onto the quiet fields where no growing stirs the soil. Only the animals and I share this day. Regardless of the date in early January when it actually occurs, this begins the Epiphany season for me, this day that is a holy time on the farm.

There is no life around the animals and me. No plants grow, no heat warms, no sap runs. We hang now by hope . . . hope that the hay and meal in the

barn are enough, faith that they are, for there is no more to be bought anywhere once ours is gone. Hope that the winter which lies just beyond the borders of the farm waiting to roll over us will be merciful, that the herd will survive with little or no loss, that the power lines which bring warmth to the chicken house will not blow down this winter, that the cats on the bleak and empty patio will stay through the winter in the shelter Sam has built for them and not abandon us for the cow-warm barn.

While we were making holiday, color and smell slipped away deep into the earth and we did not notice. Today, passing from window to window and looking out on my faded kingdom, I notice. When they return, it will be spring again, and I shall welcome them and it. For now, only hope is enough. In hope there is such rest from purpose and effort. There is nothing I can do today. Nothing I must do. Nothing to be done. Only to wait. Wait for the children to come home. Wait for the spring. Wait for the return of the plants. Wait for life. It is the day when I make memories, and there is no interruption to my play.

The quiet assembles for me the holiday that I will remember, the one I will add to my catalog of Christmases. The cooking, the shopping, the crowdedness, the tension of money are so far back into the dark December that I could not recall them now even if I had will enough to do so.

All that lies around me is what love wants to select and bring inside my heart for storage . . . Laura when the two of them opened the food processor—I did buy it and the ten-speed both, of course, borrowing against tomorrow—Sam when he brought in a box of chocolate-covered cherries from town and laid them without a word said on the counter . . . he did, however, wink at Rebecca (I saw him) . . . the spot on the velvet chair where Grandma sat on Devie's caramel and smushed it and then got stuck and everybody laughed as we scraped her free.

For all these things,
Lord, I am grateful.

For Silly Sally and her calf and all the calves and births and mamas that have followed since,
Lord, I am grateful.

For the hope of death and the promise of unending,
Lord, I am grateful.

For the children and herds and seeds to continue here after me,
Lord I am grateful.

For rituals and customs that weave me into them and them into me and all into You,
Lord, I am grateful.

The forenoon passes over into afternoon. Even the light leaves early today, having scarcely come at all in its grayness. The hours are sweet as death itself must be.

In time I hear the rumble and clatter of the school bus, the air rushing from its brakes, the slap of the red Stop sign opening, the metallic bang of the rubber-flanged door, then the voices coming up from the road, coming home from the world. I want it to go on forever—their voices and their children's voices coming home.

I open the door and hold back the storm glass as they come in.

"Hi, kids. How'd it go today?"

"Fine. What's to eat. We're starved!"

For all these things,
Lord, I am grateful.

January 6

While every European child can tell you that January 6 is the day the kings come and leave gifts for all good children, most Americans, young or old, pay only passing attention to the Epiphany. By tradition, the day celebrates the revealing of God's incarnate Self to humankind. Obviously, it first and foremost remembers God's calling of the kings to worship at the manger-cradle. Secondly, although it has been less prominently mentioned by the church over the years, January 6 is also the day when Christ's first miracle is recalled and its story retold. In turning the wedding water into wine, Our Lord revealed himself for the first time as deity.

Even allowing that most of us grow up knowing, at least intellectually, most of this, I never assigned much spiritual or private value to January 6 until fairly recently. In fact, it took a cow to make the day holy for me.

11

A LIGHT UNTO THE GENTILES

The Epiphany always comes with snow for us and the steely cold of serious winter, but last year only the cold came. It was a Tuesday, the children already back in school, Sam's patients already back to needing hospital care as well as routine checks, the manuscript load on my desk already stacking up again beyond what I could reach around without a schedule and a duty calendar. I hung one for January on the cork board above my desk and sighed. It was miserably full with no breaks until the kids' first holiday on Martin Luther King's birthday. Christmas was over all right!

The little office off the kitchen where I work was an afterthought in the mind of some previous owner and is attached only on one side to the house. The other three sides jut out like an afterthought should and are walls of windows. I like the openness, the light, the sense of being outside while I work. I can look up from my desk and see our neighbor's barn and garden. I can look south to the pond and Mary's Hill. Behind my desk the windows open east toward our barn and orchard and toward the close and cemetery beyond.

It is a comfortable vista and a comfortable room except when it's extremely cold. Then the wind finds a thousand holes around the storm glasses and the window caulking, under the door, beneath the foundation. The best index to how cold it is is not Sam's outdoor thermometer; it's the inside lower edge of my office door. If there's frost inside the door, it's cold.

Last Epiphany it was cold. The frost on my side of the door had become a layer of ice by the time I sat down to work at eight-thirty. The wind was hungry as a wild dog across the fields. I was amazed, looking toward the close, to see Buckwheat standing in the open field rather than with the herd down by the sheltering trees. Heavy with calf, she was gargantuan in the hard light of the January cold. Her back was covered with frost, her hide sparkling as each blast of wind raised the crystalline jewels on her back and held them to the light. She stood in plain view just beyond the wide gate which allows the pickup to pass from the yard and the orchard to the pastures and the barn. She could not have chosen a more vulnerable spot on so bitter a day and I found myself drawn time and again from the papers before me back to the windows behind me. There was something about her absolute stillness that was almost bothersome. At one point she lay down for a few minutes, but almost immediately she was back up and standing again stock still in the same position she had held for over an hour.

Buckwheat is easily the children's favorite cow and Sam's pet. She's also the biggest cow I have ever seen. Like Saint, she is horned and her span is a good two and a half feet across. Unlike Saint, however, she's a good-hearted beast, big enough to be gentle and generous at no expense to herself. But Buckwheat has never liked me. Certainly she's never shown hostility or threatened my right to move freely among the herd. She just doesn't like me.

Animals, like people, have their preferences, their instincts and reactions, and I would never cross them deliberately. So Buckwheat and I have developed an understanding, a kind of ladies' agreement, over the years. When I come into the pasture, she backs away and waits until I am gone. By contrast, the bull is my creature, my pet. So Bull comes to be patted and scratched and Buckwheat leaves, just like a party in the city. Simple rules; simple courtesy.

But Buckwheat, like me or not, is rarely inscrutable and almost never peculiar. Standing there on that open rise in the driving cold was peculiar. I gave it up and settled back down most unwillingly to the galleys in front of me.

In a minute I heard Buckwheat do something. It was hardly a moo, and only bulls bellow, but the sound was somewhere closer to bellow than moo. Had she been a goose, I would have said she honked, if you can imagine a one-ton honk.

In a minute the sound came again. I turned around and looked toward the gate. Just as I looked, Buckwheat lowered her head six inches, extended her neck and let out a honk to end all honks. Then she turned her head, looked straight at the office windows and waited. I stood up and went over to the window through which she could undoubtedly see my movement if not me. She honked again, this time looking right at the house and sending that distressing noise over me. Then she lowered her head to the ground and began to bob it as she licked and nuzzled the black mound of stuff on the ground in front of her.

She had calved! That dumb cow had chosen the coldest, windiest spot on the whole frozen farm to calve in! Sam had just checked her last night and she had shown no signs of being ready. Now she had done this stupid thing. I was annoyed beyond speech . . . until it dawned on me that Buckwheat is not a dumb cow. Nor is she original. She is, as a matter of fact, bright as cows go, the leader of the herd when Bull is elsewhere. But it goes against all the instincts and habits of cows to do their birthing in the open and/or especially around people, so why as near the house as she could get on top of the most exposed rise she could find?

She honked again and licked some more. The calf raised its head and lowered it. I was sorely tempted to bundle up and at least step out as far as the gate to see the size of the little fellow, but knowing Buckwheat, I knew she wouldn't like my coming that near.

She honked again. Darned cow! What in the world was wrong with her? I'd never heard such a sound in all my years with cows. In irritation I went back to my desk and passed a boring ten minutes chasing errors, mostly commas. *Why all typesetters are in love with commas beats me,* I thought as I deleted the fourth superfluous one in as many pages. Buckwheat honked. I stood up and looked out. The calf was still lying on the ground and the afterbirth had come. As I leaned toward the window to see better, Buckwheat bellowed again as if she had found a whole new line of conversation and intended to stick with it for the rest of our days together.

The phone rang and I talked, endlessly it seemed, although I can't remember now to whom or about what. It was ten-thirty already, I realized, and went to make myself some tea to warm my fingers. Buckwheat was still nuzzling and licking. Ten-thirty! That calf should be up by now. Should be nursing. Should be moving. That calf was freezing!

That was why she had come! The barn paddocks were closed because we hadn't thought it was time yet to put her up and she had done the only other possible thing. She had come for help. The most aloof and self-sufficient of the whole lot had come for help.

I watched for what seemed like hours, but by the clock was no more than a quarter of an hour. If I went out, I would have to take the calf in order to save it. Given her consistent distrust of me, she would (or so I surmised) charge me to defend the calf. Even assuming she could be cajoled—a silly assumption right from the start—the minute I picked the calf up it would have my odor even in the cold, and she would forever reject it. A motherless calf in the deep winter has less than no chance to survive, even given all the human help possible.

As if reading the space between us, Buckwheat gave one last bellow, moved away from the calf and lay down. *All right,* I thought, *a fair offer deserves a fair chance.* To leave the calf, still wet from birthing, any longer in the wind would be to lose it. If she were to charge, I would be alone. I would be the one lying in the pasture unable to escape the zero weather.

The calf did not move at all now. I could no longer detect its breathing even. Buckwheat was as silent as she had been loud. It was my decision.

I wrapped Sam's huge duck-down coat around me. I might need its warmth desperately and its thickness might absorb a horn if she only grazed me.

I went as far as the gate. Buckwheat turned her

head, looked straight at me for a full minute, and then turned away. The calf did not appear to be breathing. I opened the gate, leaving it ajar behind me for hasty retreat, and slipped over into Buckwheat's territory. She did not move. The ice on her back glittered as the sun came out briefly from behind a cloud. The meadow was quiet as death. I moved toward the calf. Nothing happened.

I stooped and put my hand out to touch its side and see if it were still breathing. As I touched, Buckwheat rose regally to her feet. For so large an animal she is graceful and agile beyond belief. She stood not ten feet from me, upright on all four feet, and looked down where I squatted beside her calf. At fifty I was large all right, but no longer agile and never graceful. And I think she thought it over. For just one portion of a second, I think she considered her advantage and then rejected it. She moved to her left upwind of me as if my odor still offended intolerably even in her hour of need. I picked up the inert calf. Safely in my arms, it opened an eye. Frozen, yes, but not yet dead.

I turned my back on Buckwheat and headed out the gate. As I turned to lock it back behind me, I looked straight into Buckwheat's face. She had followed us so stealthily that even the cracking grass had not betrayed her. I realized instantly that she could once more have had me had she wished. She hadn't wished. I locked the gate and carried the calf into the house.

Like every farmhouse ours has its sizeable supply of old blankets, spreads, sheets and rags. I gathered up two or three and wiped the motionless calf dry and then wrapped the whole thing in more blankets. Nothing happened—no sound, no movement, no twitch. I turned on the space heater and almost as quickly took off Sam's coat. It was ninety degrees in that kitchen. Still no response from the calf.

Finally, I did the only thing I knew to do. I sat down on the floor crosslegged and took Buckwheat's calf into the warmth of my body, circling it as best I could with my arms and my legs. At least I could feel it still breathing that way.

And I sat there just waiting, for what I don't know. My mind began to wander as minds do, of course. Suddenly I came back from my daydreaming and realized that I was rocking the calf and singing to it as I had sung to so many other Tickles before it. And the calf had opened her eyes. By lunch, as we sat on the floor together, she had begun to wiggle. Shortly thereafter she tried to nurse my sleeve and I knew we were home free.

I set the calf down and tried to wake up all the parts of my body that had long since even ceased to hurt. Buckwheat, when I looked out, was still standing at the gate.

The calf behind me tried to stand up and fell smack down on the slick kitchen floor. But it protested. It protested rather firmly in fact. I carried her into the carpeted office and she stood up immediately. Over the next hour she investigated the whole office, sucked on every projection, and bawled twice. She even, while I was making myself a sandwich, wobbled across the kitchen floor, negotiating it successfully this time, and made it to the living room.

A calf in the living room is like a plow on the front porch, too much even for me. I picked Covenant up. I had done the naming this time. The galleys she had interrupted by her precipitous arrival were a novel called *Covenant at Coldwater* by John Osier. The name had come to me sometime during my crooning, I suppose. I wasn't even conscious of any decision, but Covenant it was and still is.

So I picked Covenant up and out we went to the orchard. Whether she was going to be Buckwheat's now or ours to try to nourish on a bottle, we had to know. Not only was the living room too much, but she was weakening from hunger. Covenant shone dry and jet black in my arms as I carried her to the pear trees and set her down. Buckwheat watched. I went to the gate. Buckwheat stepped back as was her custom. I swung the gate wide. Still she hesitated. I moved back into the garden and she came through the untended gate into the orchard. I locked the gate behind her and left as quickly as possible.

Back into the house I went and out the front door to the back far corner of the yard from where I could watch the orchard undetected. Covenant was already nursing by the time I got there. Good! I would leave them until Sam got home. They would follow him to the barn with no prodding. The adventure, if not the day, was over, and the galleys were still waiting on my desk.

I put the rags in to wash and cleaned up the kitchen. The children would be home soon. Too late to really begin anything on my desk now. I sat down in my big desk chair and dozed for a minute.

I'd never thought much about Epiphany, never had any significant event to mark it before. The giving of the Child to the Gentiles. Certainly there had been nothing godly about my day and there would never be anything divine about Buckwheat. Yet I had never wondered before about Joseph. Why had he let the kings in? Did he need their gifts for his escape, need them to buy his Son safe passage to Egypt? Why would a Jew allow Gentile hands to touch what he must have known by then was sacred? Did need drive Joseph as it had driven Buckwheat? Did it take him to the despised and disgusting, to those whose very odor was an offense? I was fascinated by my dozing reverie.

The bell rang. Kids home and loud from school. No more thoughts until after supper when, the calf and her mama safely in the barn and the house quiet around us, I blew out the Christ Candle for the last time till next Christmas. As I did, I said to Sam, "Thank goodness we never have everything we need without having to ask each other."

"Thinking about Buckwheat and Covie?" he asked smiling.

"Yeah," I said. "I never rocked a calf before," but really I was thinking of Joseph and how the light came to the Gentiles.

Photo by Sam Tickle

Phyllis A. Tickle is Senior Editor of St. Luke's Press and Poet-in-Residence of Brooks Gallery in Memphis, Tennessee. She was awarded an M.A. degree from Furman University, Greenville, South Carolina.

Among Mrs. Tickle's published works are *Selections: A Retrospective Collection of Poetry, Tobias and the Angel, On Beyond AIS, American Genesis*. Her poetry has been included in many anthologies and her columns and book reviews appear regularly in a number of magazines. She is an active member of the Episcopalian laity and a frequent contributor to the publications of the church.

The author lives with her husband Sam and the three of their seven children still at home on a farm near Lucy, Tennessee.